Data Models for Banking, Finance, and Insurance

JUMPSTART DATABASE DESIGNS WITH PROVEN PATTERNS

"You're the expert! Design me a database!"
Mid-level Manager at Morgan Stanley

Claire L. Frankel

Technics Publications
SEDONA, ARIZONA

Published by:

115 Linda Vista, Sedona, AZ 86336 USA

https://www.TechnicsPub.com

Edited by R. Raymond McGirt

First Printing 2024

ISBN, print ed.   9781634625081
ISBN, Kindle ed.   9781634625104
ISBN, PDF ed.   9781634623827

Library of Congress Control Number: 2024943761

Dedicated to the memory of Hariharan ("Harry") Sinniah, 1966-2016

Data Modeler Extraordinaire

Thank You

Jamie Knowles at Idera, Inc. for supporting this book from the beginning and supplying the license for ER/Studio.

Thank You

Steve Hoberman for being open to every idea.

Thank You

Contents

ONE

Design Pattern Fundamentals

Introduction

Anyone who thinks they can use these models 'as is' has not spoken with their business End Users!

This book provides introductory and baseline Entity Relationship Diagrams (ERDs) for building your relational database. Augment and expand these baseline models with the input received from your business users as they describe their unique financial environment. When your user's input has been added and agreed upon, it is time to review the Logical ERD with your Database Administrators (DBAs) and discuss what is necessary to make them Physical (housekeeping attributes, input and output considerations, etc.).

A complete Physical ERD, with all of the housekeeping and any Physical entities in place, can be used to produce first cut Data Definition Language (DDL) code targeted to any relational database. For the scoping of modeling within this book, banking, finance, and insurance companies means:

- Banking is the practice of a financial institution licensed to accept deposits, manage withdrawals, and make loans.

- Finance is a term that refers to the management, creation, and study of money and investments. It uses credit, debt, securities, and other investments to fund current projects using future income flows.

- Insurance (from Oxford Languages) is a practice or arrangement by which a company or government agency provides a guarantee of compensation for specified loss, damage, illness, or death in return for payment of a premium.

In this book, we will discuss data modeling templates for these five loosely defined business areas by developing these models:

- Retail and Commercial Banking ('Banking')
- Credit Cards ('Banking')
- Securities, Investments, and Brokerage ('Investments')
- Capital and Financial Markets ('Finance')

- Property, Casualty, and Life Insurance ('Insurance')

The purpose of the data modeling templates for these five business areas is to save you start-up time when embarking on a database design assignment. They will save project time by giving you a jump-start into the most widely used topics (subject areas).

This book assumes an intermediate knowledge of data modeling. Although some basic definitions are provided, we will not explain the concept of an entity, attribute, or relationship. You have to know this stuff first.

If you are not familiar with data modeling or if your skills are a bit rusty, please read Steve Hoberman's book, "Data Modeling Made Simple".

To build a full-fledged attributed and defined database, you will also need, in addition to knowledge of data modeling, a sophisticated tool, such as Erwin or ER/Studio. These tools may not seem as sophisticated as Collibra or Alation but whoa! Wait until you start reverse engineering, comparing data dictionaries, establishing lineage, and governance! There are capabilities in these two tools that will astound you!

Define the Business Needs

This book provides templates to help you jump start your database design. Whether you want to create self-contained 'masterfiles' (a collection of entities or subject areas of importance to the business and used repeatedly by the business), or databases to service an entire enterprise, these starter, editable templates are intended to save you weeks of discussions with your End Users and business managers.

The templates enable you to review the entities and attributes with your users and managers. They can say "yes" or "no" to a proposed entity or an entire subject area. They can also suggest modifications, additions, and subtractions.

Before you select your first template at the Conceptual and Logical levels, you must define your organization's needs. In other words, what is the goal of this masterfile, enterprise database, or set of databases? An organization that needs to capture family assets and family relationships between customers will require a different database design from an options trading database...even when the customers are the same people.

Be sure to meet with the owner(s) paying the bill for this endeavor. You do not want to get to the final Logical model walk-through only to discover that corporate management has a different vision of the business. Of course, you can expect to uncover a few changes in any walk-through, but not changes to the whole model (unless your funding is suddenly dropped from the budget).

This brings us to communication, communication, communication. To nail down the goal and anticipated usage of your database, you MUST meet with:

- The senior business managers who will be paying for the database.
- The mid-level managers who define projects and influence the senior people.
- The business analysts who capture (and write up) business needs and goals.
- The data stewards who know how the data is structured.

Hopefully, these meetings will take place in one big group. Take careful, dated notes (publish them), and always run your conclusions by these four groups after each meeting. You want their support and buy-in.

Do Not Promise to Boil the Ocean

In other words, if senior staff is talking about an enterprise-wide database/application to address every single one of their issues (perhaps with some new or soon-to-be-released technology), you are advised to talk with them about "do-able deliverables" within a certain time frame. Offer them a choice of alternatives, such as a phased approach, with small deliverables in each business quarter. Do not allow yourself and your team t o be trapped in an enormous deliverable with a fixed deadline, resulting in working all hours of the day and night.

Do not interpret the above paragraph as my opposition to an enterprise-wide database. I am very much in favor of enterprise databases. However, as practical engineers, we must realize that enterprise-anything does not get built in three weeks. A beginning outline is more practical at three months, initial (not all) subject areas complete nine months later, and a team to grow and maintain the enterprise starship for many future budget cycles. As your business grows and changes over the years, it is wise to keep the same enterprise team in place to rock and roll with the business! You do this by rewarding them!

An engineering plan endorsed by senior management can be your ticket to success. For example, at a high level:

- Year 1, Basic Functionally—e.g., Basic Customer and Product entities
- Year 2, Intermediate Functionality—e.g., The ability to process some transactions
- Year 3, Advanced Functionality—e.g., Processing all transactions for a given department

About Data Modeling Tools

Many tools in the marketplace, developed in the US and Europe, claim to be data modeling tools. Some of them will give you the functionality of just a drawing tool. Avoid using just drawing tools, no matter how inexpensive, because there is no connectivity between model levels (Conceptual to Logical to Physical) and they are not capable of producing DDL. Plus, the ability to reverse engineer databases may be crucial for your success, and drawing tools provides no pathways to reverse engineer.

Always use a comprehensive data modeling tool, such as Erwin or ER/Studio. What do we mean by "a comprehensive data modeling tool?" This is a tool that can support each type of data model–Conceptual, Logical, and Physical ERDs, as well as star schemas. The tool can generate DDL, reverse engineer a database, and offer its own dictionary or storage for definitions of each data object, each data type, supporting reference notes, and all associated material, including code fragments. Some tools also allow a direct connection to the database engine.

As a data Modeler, your goal is to deliver to the DBAs a "first cut" of DDL. In other words, an almost-ready-for-production database - ready for mounting onto the target database and some production tuning for that target.

Tools that will only let you draw a diagram are useless in producing a production-ready database.

Middle and End User Expertise

Even if your users are not all that familiar with technology, they have a body of knowledge you need to draw on for the success of your design. It is the business detail, business flow, and business comprehension that you seek. Start with these templates, particularly for Customer and Product, and discover how they relate to your business. Ask about all the details a business person must know to get the Product into the Customer's hands.

In a typical financial corporation, you have different types of users. You have senior people who have an overall vision of the business. You have End Users who support orders and solve customer issues on their terminals. You have mid-level users who catch problems, define business requirements, and recommend improved processing procedures. When designing a model for a particular application, these people are theoretically available to help you define data items, entities, and attributes. It may be challenging to schedule their time because they have their own day-job to accomplish. However, it is very important to obtain their input.

There may be no one available to write a Requirements Document. If this is the case, you need to create a draft document to serve as a guidepost to what is known and what is unknown. Share this document after every addition of new information. You will need an official signoff after completing the requirements. The Requirements Document can function as a contract between you (the IT representative/specialist) and the business, especially regarding your deliverables and due dates. Include a draft schedule along with the Requirements Document. Try to get senior management's signature before doing too much work. If they are not available to sign, simply copy them on intermediate and complete Requirements Documentation and all project plans.

From Conceptual, Logical, and Physical Models to First Cut DDL

This book will focus on templates for Conceptual, Logical, and Physical Data Models/ERDs. We will also see a sample Logical star schema.

You can modify each template for your unique business. If all you do is grab a Physical model template and try to implement it, you will get lost in the weeds (of terminology, mapping to sources, relationships, etc.) So, start with Conceptual, please.

TWO

Conceptual Models for Financial Services

Model 1.0: The Fundamental Conceptual Model

The Fundamental Conceptual Model for all businesses is

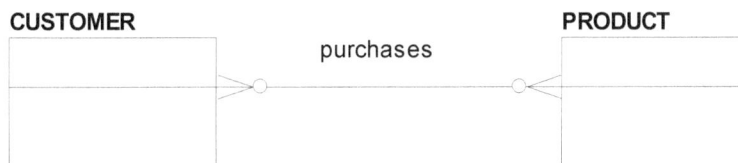

Model 1.0: Customer <purchases> Product

You can think of this ERD as the basic imperative. Every single transaction in the business world boils down to a customer purchasing a product, whether that Product is a bank account, a share of stock, an insurance policy, or a service such as 24-hour monitoring of an account.

This fundamental ERD is represented as: Customer as an entity and Product as an entity. Their relationship is Customer may purchase many Products (active voice) and a Product may be purchased by many Customers (passive voice). It is a many-to-many relationship. As a reminder, cardinality is the numerical relationship between rows of one table and rows in another. Common cardinalities include one-to-one, one-to-many, and many-to-many. The Customer and Product entities here represent subject areas containing extensive entities and attributes; we will enumerate them in Logical modeling. Definitions for each of these entities:

- **Customer**– A legal entity with the authority to sign contracts, open a financial account and transact business in the financial account; a person over the age of 18 or 21 (depending on the State or Country), or a Corporation, a Company which has filed a DBA ("Doing Business As"), a Trust or other legal entity recognized by the Courts.

- **Product**– An item or service offered for sale in a marketplace. Financial instruments, such as savings accounts, stock, bonds and insurance policies are examples of Products. Note that financial advice, contracted from a brokerage firm or registered representative, is also a Product.

A basic Conceptual ERD consists only of boxes, lines, and definitions. That is, boxes are entities, which we then think of as subject areas (for all of the information they will contain in the future), and lines are relationships. It is handy to have definitions of the entities along with relationships, right in the Conceptual Model. It fosters agreement on the definition of things between their human managers!

In the Conceptual Model, most relationships are many-to-many. Each entity must have a name describing the subject area as a whole and the data type to be collected. We should name each relationship in a Conceptual Model in at least one direction–the most active direction (i.e., the entity acting upon another entity).

A business's Conceptual Model should contain no more than 20 entities. More than 20 entities and your business people may be trying to "boil the ocean." In other words, they may be trying to anticipate a database that would solve every single problem the company faces; it is an enormous or rapidly expanding scope of work which will be very difficult to deliver in a reasonable time frame. This is not practical. If you are faced with a Conceptual Model which has grown to more than 25 entities, STOP! Go back to the basic computing needs of the business. Determine what can be in-scope for this project's cost and timeframe, and what has to be "out of scope" or scheduled for later development. Extra entities may also signal the presence of more detail (and not necessarily a broader scope). The extra detail may belong in the Logical Model and not in the Conceptual.

Present 10-20 entities in a Conceptual Model to senior management and get their buy-in. If senior management has committed to 'databases for the world,' introduce a phased approach to divide and conquer the assignment.

 If key personnel are insisting on more entities at the Conceptual level, it may not necessarily mean a broader scope; it may be that those entities belong at the Logical level. Praise the people for thinking ahead and add the entities to a draft Logical Model.

Model 2.0: Conceptual Model for Financial Services: Retail and Commercial Banking

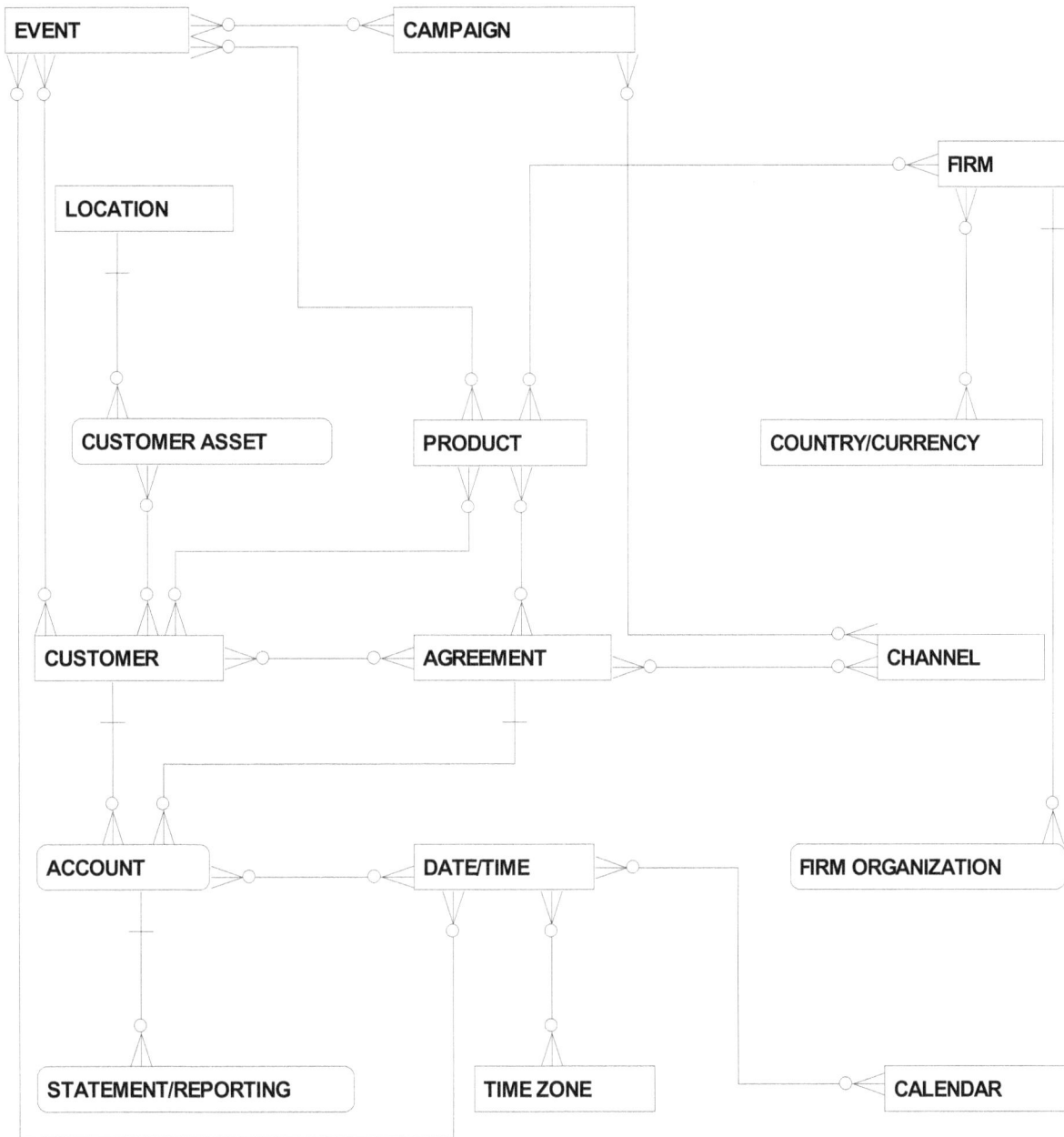

Model 2.0: Conceptual Model for Financial Services: Retail and Commercial Banking

Above is a basic Conceptual ERD using ER/Studio (entities only); the entity definitions are below.

Customer	Product	Account	Agreement
Location	Firm	Firm Organization	Event
Customer	Asset	Campaign	Channel
Statement/Reporting		Calendar	Date/Time

Reference entities: *Country/Currency, Exchange, and Time Zone. More on these later.*

Definitions: You may modify these definitions in accordance with the business understanding of the term. Typically, we store a definition for each entity and attribute in a designated definitions field in your data modeling tool.

- **Customer**–a legal entity with the authority to sign contracts; a person over the age of 18 or 21 (depending on the state or country), a corporation, a company which has filed a Doing business as; a trust or other legal entity recognized by the courts.

- **Product**–a Physical or non-Physical object offered for sale in a marketplace. A service offered for sale is also a product. Examples: cars, nuts and bolts, financial instruments such as stock, bonds, and insurance policies, 24-hour standby maintenance service.

- **Agreement**–A contract to perform the sale or usage of a product and/or the delivery of a service between two or more legal entities. Examples: insurance policy, financial advisor contract, and credit card usage terms.

- **Account**–A record in either virtual and/or Physical form of a specific type of transaction between two legal entities, usually based upon an initial Agreement. Examples: bank account, brokerage account. Note: An agreement may result in the establishment of several different types of accounts, but an account belongs to one agreement.

- **Location**–Comprehensive information for making contact with the legal entity;. Includes Physical addresses, telephone and fax numbers, email addresses, other internet-based addresses, URLs, etc.

- **Firm**–A firm is a business organization that seeks to make a profit through the sale of goods and services. The term firm is synonymous with business or company. Firms can operate under several different structures, including sole proprietorships and corporations.

- **Firm Organization/Org Chart**–A data model representation of the organization chart/structure of a firm, including employee name, employee title, level in the firm, responsibilities, and other information pertinent to the business.

- **Customer Asset**–An item of value owned by a Customer. Examples: a home, a building, funded accounts with various firms, cars, boats, jewelry, etc.

- **Event**–An occurrence of importance to the business, and which may result in a change to a Customer's assets or account. An Event may also be of importance to the firm itself, whether or not it affects Customer accounts, such as a change in Management structure.

- **Campaign**–An organized activity for a specified purpose, usually to increase sales. Example: a campaign to air six Coca-Cola ads during the Superbowl.

- **Channel**–The method by which information is transmitted. In the case of the Superbowl ads, the channel is television, specifically CBS or FOX will carry the traditional broadcast of the game and Nickelodeon will air an exclusive kids- and family-friendly telecast. The CBS or FOX broadcast will be available to stream via Paramount+.

- **Statement/Reporting**–A printed or virtual report of account transactions for a specific period of time, usually a month, a quarter or a year.

- **Country/Currency**–One of the reference entities, not shown in every model, but added when necessary. This reference entity contains a chart or charts of valid country names, country abbreviations, the ISO two and three character country codes, their associated currency (monetary form), and valid currency abbreviations including ISO codes in accordance with ISO 4217.

- **Exchange**–Exchange is one of the reference entities, not shown in every model, but added when necessary. Exchange information may be required for some brokerage applications. Exchange is the marketplace where securities are traded. Examples are the New York Stock Exchange (NYSE) and NASDAQ.

- **Time Zone**–Time Zone is one of the reference entities not shown in every model but added when necessary. This information may be necessary for international applications. Time Zones are measured from Greenwich, U.K. Each Time Zone also has a unique name such as Eastern Time or Greenwich Mean Time.

- **Calendar**–One of the reference entities, it is a chart or series of pages showing the days, weeks, and months of a particular year. Accounting calendars determine the accounting period to which a financial transaction will be booked.

- **Date/Time**–In Financial Services Date/Time usually refers to the calendar date and time at location (the Date/Time stamp) affixed to a piece of data when it initially enters the firm.

Model 3.0: Conceptual Model for Credit Cards

The Credit Card Conceptual model will cover the state of entering customer information, maintaining charges and payments, and producing monthly statements, which is the regular daily business of managing credit cards in a financial institution.

It will not cover prospecting for new customers or conducting sales campaigns via various channels. It will also not cover deleting credit card customers for various reasons, such as fraud.

To help think this through, note that a Product has a subtype of Banking Product and a Credit Card is one of many Banking Product(s).

An Agreement has a subtype of Application; a Credit Application is a particular type of Application.

An Agreement has a relationship with Agreement Access Device, while a Credit Card is the vehicle which enables credit to be used.

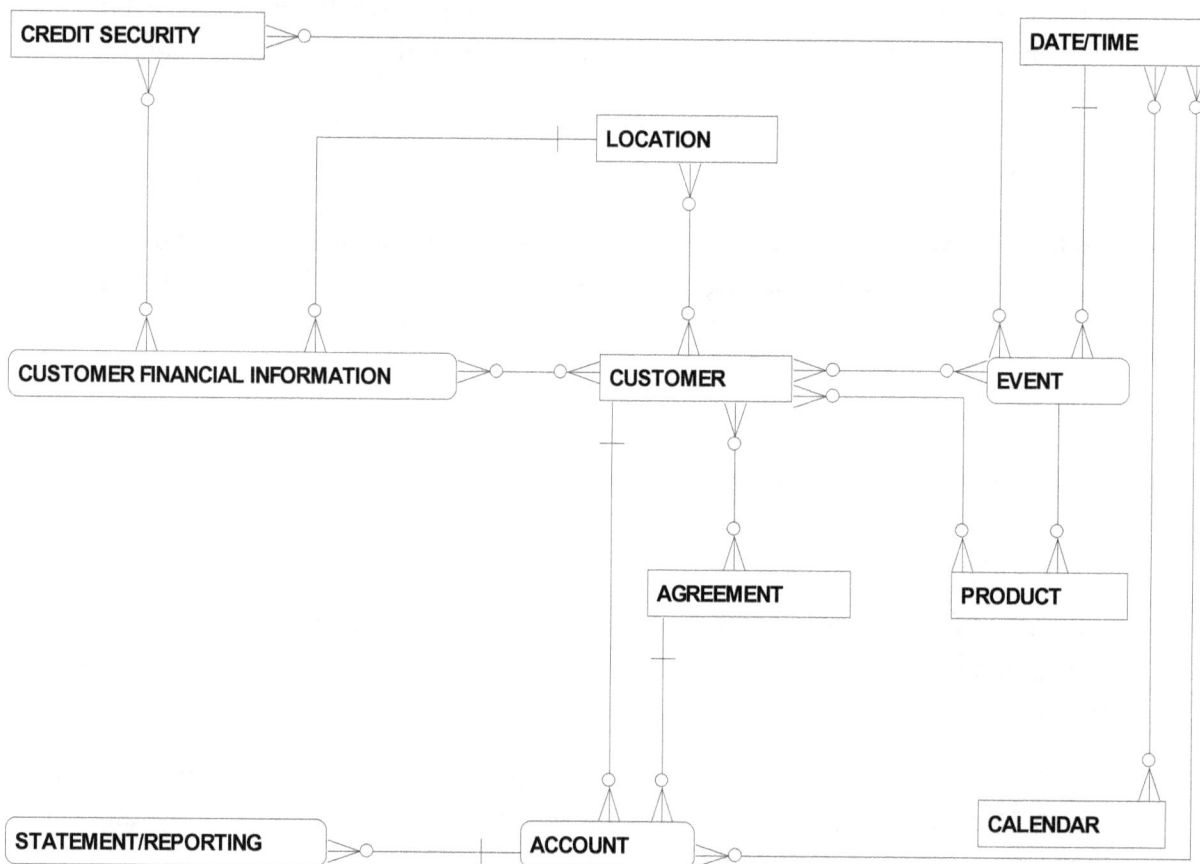

Model 3.0: Conceptual Model for Credit Cards

The definitions for these entities exist in the prior model: Customer, Product, Location, Statement/Reporting, Calendar, Date/Time, and Agreement.

<u>Definitions </u>for new entities are here:

Customer Financial Information/ Risk Calculation–Lenders use the 5 Cs of credit analysis to assess the level of risk associated with lending to a particular individual or company. By evaluating the legal entity's character, capacity, capital, collateral, and conditions, lenders can determine the likelihood of the borrower repaying the loan on time and in full.

Security–Credit card security is intended to protect the owner from transactions due to theft of the credit card and/or its information. The top five methods for securing a credit card are:

- EMV chip technology. EMV technology stands for Europay, MasterCard, and Visa
- Contactless payment
- PIN (Personal Identification Number)
- CVV (Card Verification Value)
- Two-factor authentication (2FA)

Model 4.0: Conceptual Model for Capital and Financial Markets

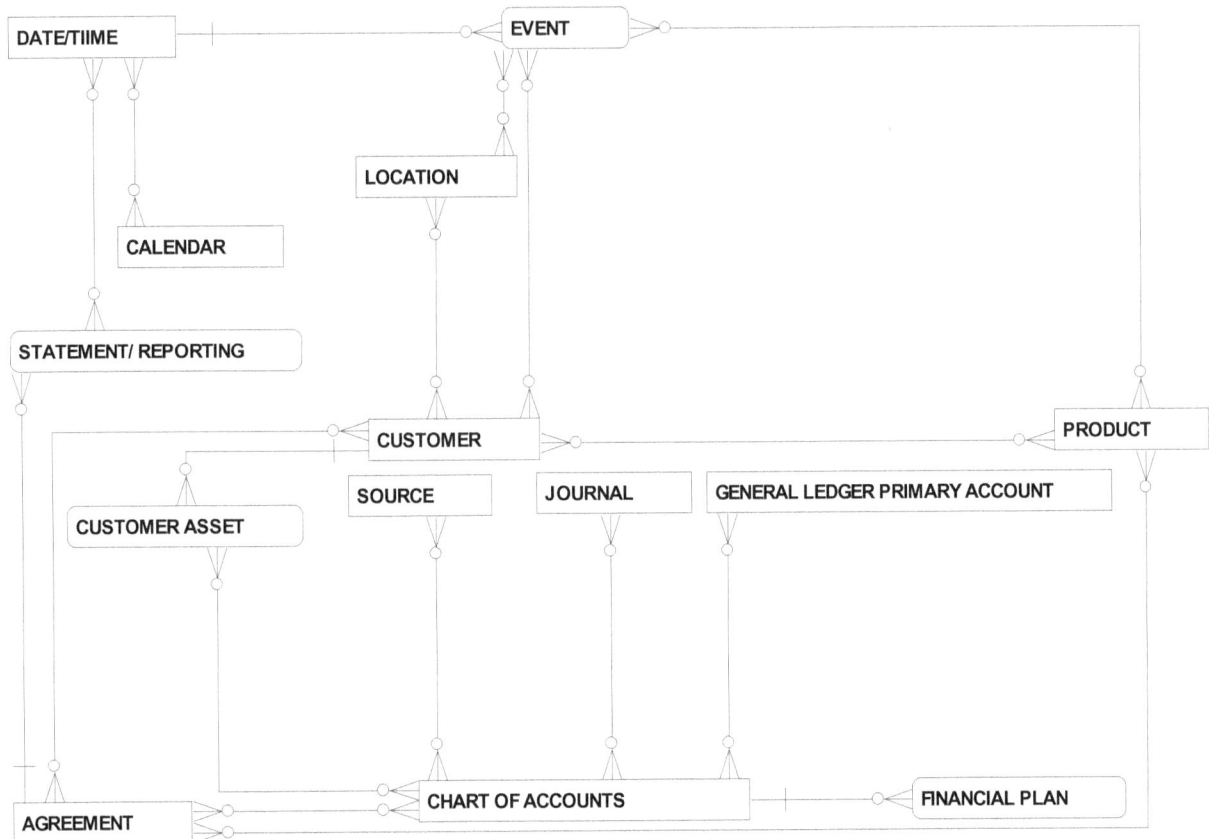

<u>Model 4.0:</u> Conceptual Model for Capital and Financial Markets

The definitions for these entities exist in a prior model: Customer, Product, Location, Event, Agreement, Calendar, Date/Time, and Statement/Reporting.

Definitions for new entities include:

- **General Ledger/ Primary Account**–The main accounting record of a company or organization. Family Offices (Private Wealth Management) may also maintain a General Ledger.

- **Source**–The originating system, person, or organization for transaction information; a supplier of information or capital. Further, in investments and brokerage, a source is typically an exchange or market price provider.

- **Financial Plan**–A document detailing a company's or a person's current financial situation and long-term monetary goals, as well as strategies to achieve short- and long-term goals.

- **Chart of Accounts**–A financial organizational tool that provides an index of every unique record for each type of asset, liability, equity, revenue, and expense in an accounting system. This provides an insight into all the financial transactions of the company.

- **Journal**–A journal is a detailed record of all of a person's or a business's financial transactions. It is used to reconcile accounts and is transferred to other accounting records, such as the general ledger. The journal states the date of a transaction, which accounts were affected, and the dollar amounts, usually in a double-entry bookkeeping method.

Model 5.0: Conceptual Model for Securities, Investments, and Brokerage

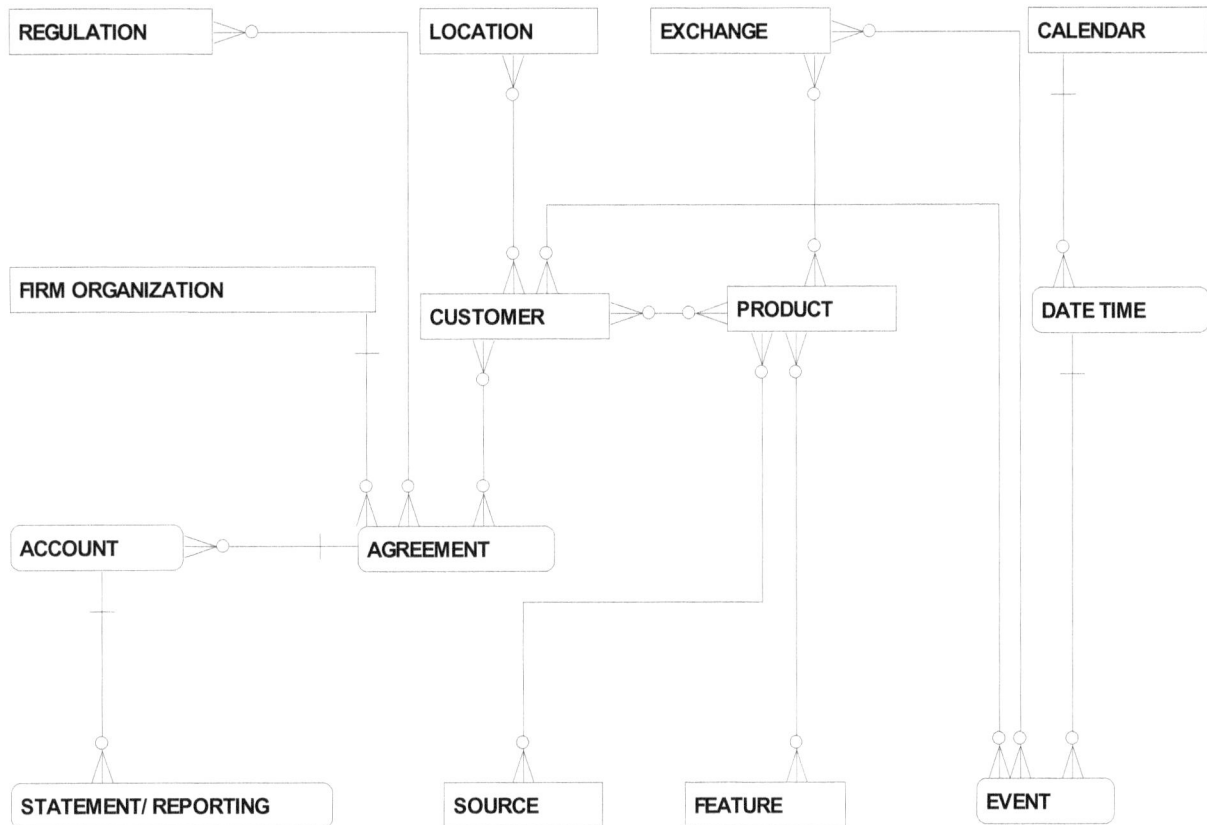

Model 5.0: Conceptual Model for Securities, Investments, and Brokerage

Definitions for the following entities can be found in previous models: Customer, Location, Source, Product (which in this case is an Instrument), Statement/Reporting, Calendar, Date/Time, and Agreement.

Definitions for new entities are:

- **Feature**–A detailed characteristic of a banking, insurance, or investment instrument, such as dividend yield or option expiration date.

- **Firm Organization/Representative**–The Org Chart shows the internal structure of an organization or company by title and reporting level. The employees and positions are represented by boxes or other shapes, and can include contact information, email, title, and other information. Straight or elbowed lines link the levels together. Representative is important because this person is the Firm's intermediary between the Customer and their Account(s), and the Firm and the Markets (Exchanges). Representative may be at the lowest level on the Org Chart or mid-level.

- **Regulation**–Financial regulation refers to the laws and rules firms operating in the Financial Industry, such as those banks, credit unions, insurance companies, financial brokers, and asset managers must follow. In the US, banks are regulated by:

  o The Office of the Comptroller of the Currency (OCC)
  o The Federal Reserve System
  o The Federal Deposit Insurance Corporation (FDIC)

  Brokerage or trading accounts, and the exchanges are regulated by

  o The Securities and Exchange Commission (SEC)
  o Financial Industry Regulatory Authority (FINRA)
  o Securities Investor Protection Corporation (SIPC)

  The insurance companies are regulated by the National Association of Insurance Commissioners (NAIC) plus an insurance regulatory agency in each U.S. state.

Model 6.0: Conceptual Model for Property, Casualty, and Life Insurance

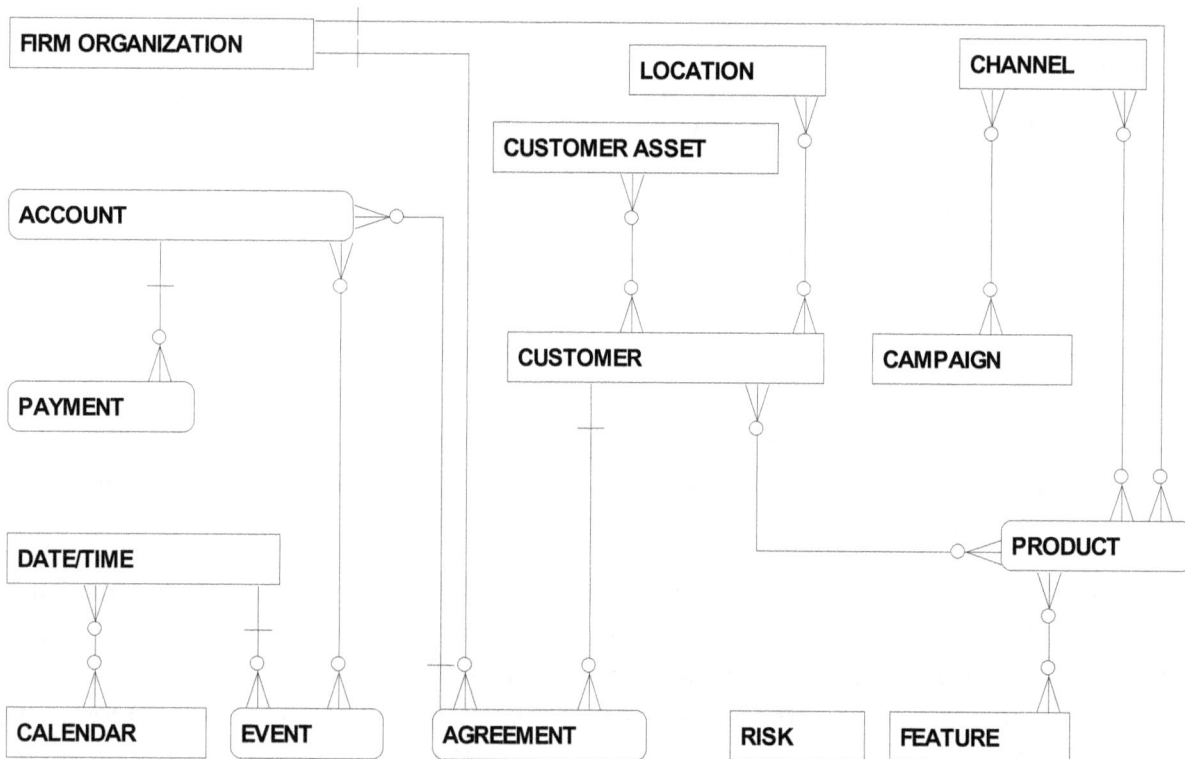

Model 6.0: Conceptual Model for Property, Casualty, and Life Insurance

Here is the basic Conceptual ERD using ER/Studio with the following entities:

Customer	Agreement	Account
Product	Date/Time	Payment
Event	Location	Customer Asset
Campaign	Channel	Calendar
Firm Organization (Rep)	Feature	Risk

All of these entities have been defined above. The understanding here is that Product is an insurance policy.

In the Logical model, we will realize that a Payment is a type of Event, not something separate.

There are strong similarities among many of these Conceptual models. Each one includes entities for Product, Customer, Agreement, Account, Event, Location, Date/Time, and Calendar. Logical modeling will expose differences in detail.

Conduct model reviews while building your Conceptual Model. A model review is simply a short presentation of the entities, their definitions and their relationships in the model and subsequent discussion as to its correctness. Inviting representation from all your user groups to model reviews is important. Always invite senior management, regardless of whether they can attend. After the model review, summarize and send minutes with agreed upon ERDs, and copy senior management.

Do not invite your DBAs to model reviews of Conceptual models, as they will die of boredom. Invite them to review late-stage Logical models and definitely all Physical models.

Notes on Reference Entities

A reference entity (representing a table) is a lookup for base objects such as a country list. They are called reference entities because every application needs and uses them.

Even if your company is not international and your customers do not do banking overseas, some of the following entities are important to incorporate into your data model and subsequent database, if only for the differences in US time zones. When they are accurately detailed in the Logical and Physical models, there will be no violations of settlement times or policy end dates. The following entities should be incorporated into every data model unless you know they will be unnecessary for the next several decades. In some industries, there may be discussions about the possibility and/or probability of new regulations. Having "stubs" or holding entities in your data model in anticipation of new regulations is not a bad idea.

- **Calendar**–The accounting calendar determines the accounting period to which a financial transaction will be booked. Every financial transaction references an accounting date and its obligation. Likewise, the settlement calendar in brokerage counts out the 1, 3 or 5 day settlement period for a trade and allows the trade to be shown as 'cleared' when the settlement period is up (and shares and cash exchange hands). Calendars also indicate the various holidays in the US and other countries; no business or limited business can be conducted on those dates. Calendar has many more uses in financial services; the above are just two examples.

- **Country/Currency**–The Country entity stores every country on every continent, their abbreviations and their associated official currency. Currency exchange is also facilitated in this subject area.

- **Time Zone**–Any of the 38 divisions of the Earth's surface used to determine the local time for any given locality. For example, New York City is in the Eastern Standard Time (EST) zone, while London is in the Greenwich Mean Time (GMT) zone.

- **Date/Time**–A mechanism for ascertaining the exact occurrence of an event. For example, the date/time stamp on a transaction (e.g., sale of stock) tells us exactly which calendar unit the transaction occurred in and at what time of day.

- **Exchange**–A government-approved and regulated marketplace for conducting financial transactions/buys and sells.

THREE

Customer and Product Logical Models

In Logical modeling, there are no restrictions on the number of entities, attributes, and relationships necessary to completely define and describe the business scope. Here we must be mindful of actually sticking to the business scope.

These Logical models will focus on the Customer and Product entities from the Conceptual first. We call them Logical subject areas and expand them into Logical templates because they are foundational to all businesses.

The Customer subject area describes an individual person, an official family/group, a company, or an organization. In other words, it is a legal entity capable of entering into business agreements and signing contracts.

The Customer subject area must encompass the actual Customer themselves, whether it is a person, company, or organization. Depending on the type of business, this subject area may also include:

- Related family members (for Private Wealth Management or Family Offices)

- An organizational chart with roles for each member (for Asset Management assignments)

- Relationships between corporations, each identified as a Customer (for Clearance and Settlement of Trades).

Notes on Logical entities and attributes:

- To qualify as a real business entity, you must identify at least two attributes defining it.

- When you see a primary key (PK) of two or more attributes, the extra attributes are necessary to establish uniqueness for that PK.

- All entities used in models here are defined in the Appendix; the only attribute definitions provided here are the more obscure ones. The list of possible values for some attributes includes examples of attribute types and the possible roles or activities they are assigned.

Customer Logical Model

The Logical Data Model for Customer–a Person, Family Group (Household), Organization, Corporation, or other legal entity includes 22 entities for the following business facts, where they exist as facts:

Customer	Customer Salutation
Customer Identification	Customer Name
Customer Related	Customer Role
Status	Customer/Status
Location	Customer/Location
Customer Financial/KYC*	Individual
Individual Name	Household
Household Member	Organization
Internal Organization	Government
Business	Association
Financial Institution	SEC Classification
Customer Asset	Customer Description

* KYC is the abbreviation for 'Know Your Customer.' It is the FINRA rule for gathering enough financial information about a customer in an effort to prevent fraud. This is defined in the Appendix under 'Customer Financial Document/ KYC.'

For definitions of these entities, not previously defined, see the Appendix.

On the next page, **Model 7.0** Customer Logical Model/ ERD is too small to read and so it is divided it into two pieces which follow:

Left side first, **Model 7.01** on page 24, then right side, **Model 7.02**, on page 25.

CUSTOMER ROLE

Customer Role ID

Customer Role Description
Customer Role Type Code
Customer Role Start Date
Customer Role End Date
Role Legal Appointment Document

SEC CLASSIFICATION

SEC Classification ID

SEC Classification Education Code (FK)
SEC Classification Employer
SEC Classification Occupation Code (FK)

CUSTOMER RELATED

Customer ID (FK)
Customer Role ID (FK)
Customer Related ID (FK)
Customer Related Role Code (FK)
Customer Related Start Date

Customer Related End Date
Customer Structure Type (FK)
Customer Related Reason Code (FK)
Customer Related Status Type Code (FK)

CUSTOMER

Customer ID

Customer Description
Customer Start Date
Customer End Date
Customer Subtype Code (FK)
Customer Type Code (FK)
Customer Initial Data Source Type Code (FK)
GDPR/CCPA Eligible YN
SEC Classification ID (FK)

CUSTOMER/LOCATION

Customer ID (FK)
Location ID (FK)
Customer Address Usage Type Code (FK)
Customer Address Start Date

Customer Address End Date

LOCATION

Location ID

Location Subtype Code (FK)

CUSTOMER SALUTATION

Customer Salutation ID
Customer ID (FK)

Customer Salutation Code

TIME ZONE

Location ID (FK)

Time Zone Name
UTC Official Time

ADDRESS

Address ID (FK)

Address Subtype Code (FK)

ROLE SPECIAL INSTRUCTION

Customer Role ID (FK)
Role Special Instruction ID

Role Special Instruction Description
Role Special Instruction From Date
Role Special Instruction To Date

HOUSEHOLD

Household ID (FK)

Household Title
Household Count
Household Child Count
Household Financial Manager Name
Household Financial Manager Employer
Household Financial Goal 1
Household Financial Goal 2
Household Financial Goal 3
Auto Support Payment Monthly
Auto Support Individual Name

CUSTOMER FINANCIAL DOCUMENT/KYC

Customer ID (FK)
Financial Document Start Date
Customer Document Type Id (FK)
Data Source Type Code (FK)

Financial Document End Date
Financial Document Id (FK)
Financial Document Time Period Code (FK)

HOUSEHOLD MEMBER

Household ID (FK)
Individual ID (FK)
Household Member Datetime

Household Member Type Code
Household Member Type Description

STREET ADDRESS

Street Address ID (FK)

Address Line 1 Text
Address Line 2 Text
Address Line 3 Text
Dwelling Type Code (FK)
City Name
State Name
Country ID (FK)
Territory Name
Postal Code ID (FK)
Carrier Route Text

INDIVIDUAL

Individual ID (FK)

Birth Date
Death Date
Gender Type Code (FK)
Tax Bracket Code (FK)
VIP Type Code (FK)
Employment Start Date
Retirement Date
Primary Account Administrator YN
Account Decision Maker YN

INDIVIDUAL NAME

Individual ID (FK)

First Name
Middle Name 1
Middle Name 2
Family Name
Suffix
Nickname
Maiden Name
Alternate Name
Individual Full Name

TELEPHINE NUMBER

Telephone Number ID (FK) (FK)

Area Code
Exchange Number
Line Number
Extension Number

CUSTOMER CREDIT RATING

Customer Credit Rating ID
Customer ID (FK)

Customer Credit Rating
Customer Credit Rating Datetime
Credit Reporting Agency Code (FK)

ORGANIZATION

Organization ID (FK)

Organization Legal Name
Organization Short Name
Organization Purpose
Organization Type Code FK)
Organization Subtype Code (FK)
Organization Established Date
Organization Closed Date
Parent Organization ID (FK)
Legal Classification Code (FK)
Ownership Type Code (FK)
DUNS ID
BIC Business Code (FK)
NAICS Sumber
Organization Fiscal Month Number
Organization Fiscal Day Number
Basel Organization Type Code (FK)
Basel Market Participant Code (FK)
Basel Eligible Central Indicator YN
Basel Business Code (FK)

OVERSEAS MILITARY ADDRESS

Overseas Military Address ID (FK)

Overseas Military Postal Code ID (FK)
Overseas Military City ID (FK)
Overseas Military Territory ID (FK)

POST OFFICE BOX ADDRESS

Post Office Box ID (FK)

Post Office Box Number
City ID (FK)
Country ID (FK)
Postal Code ID (FK)
Territory ID (FK)

CUSTOMER ASSET

Customer Asset ID
Customer ID (FK)

Customer Asset Description
Customer Asset Type Code
Customer Asset Value

CUSTOMER IDENTIFICATION

Customer Identification ID (FK)
Issuing Party ID
Customer Identification Type Code (FK)
Customer ID Start Date

Customer Id End Date
Customer Identification Alphanumeric

ELECTRONIC ADDRESS

Electromnic Address ID (FK)

Electromnic Address Subtype Code (FK)
Electromnic Address Text
Electronic Address Domain Name
Domain Root Code (FK)

INTERNAL ORGANIZATION

Organization ID (FK)

Internal Organization Type Code
Internal Organization Subtype Code
Internal Organization Number

STATUS

Status ID

Status Code
Status Description

BUSINESS

Business ID (FK)

Business Legal Start Date
Business Legal End Date
Stock Exchange Listed Ind YN
Business Category Code (FK)
Tax Bracket Code (FK)

INTERNET PROTOCOL ADDRESS

Electromnic Address ID (FK)
Internet Protocol Address ID

Internet Protocol Address Number
Internet Protocol Address ID (FK)
Internet Protocol Address Registered by Party ID (FK)
Internet Protocol Network Name

FINANCIAL INSTITUTION

Financial Institution ID (FK)

Financial Institution Type Code (FK)
Financial Institution Industry Assigned Number

CUSTOMER /STATUS

Customer ID (FK)
Customer Status ID (FK)
Customer Status Start Date

Customer Status End Date
Customer Status Code
Customer Status Reason Code (FK)

GOVERNMENT

Organization ID (FK)

Government Unit Type Code
Government Unit Description

ASSOCIATION

Association ID (FK)

Association Type Code
Association Type Description

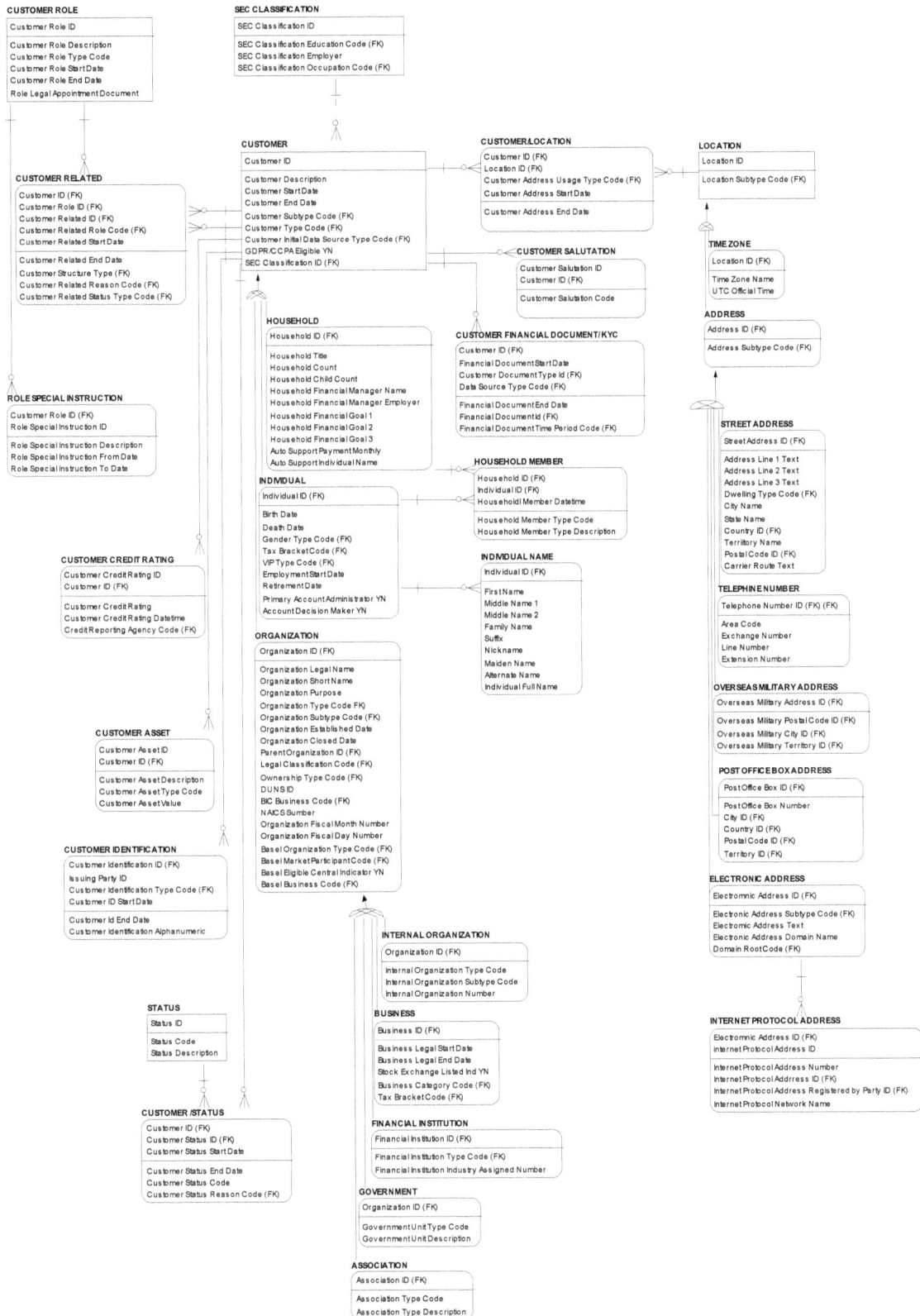

Model 7.0 Customer LDM

CUSTOMER CREDIT RATING

Customer Credit Rating ID
Customer ID (FK)

Customer Credit Rating
Customer Credit Rating Datetime
Credit Reporting Agency Code (FK)

CUSTOMER ROLE

Customer Role ID

Customer Role Description
Customer Role Type Code
Customer Role Start Date
Customer Role End Date
Role Legal Appointment Document

CUSTOMER ASSET

Customer Asset ID
Customer ID (FK)

Customer Asset Description
Customer Asset Type Code
Customer Asset Value

CUSTOMER IDENTIFICATION

Customer Identification ID (FK)
Issuing Party ID
Customer Identification Type Code (FK)
Customer ID Start Date

Customer Id End Date
Customer Identification Alphanumeric

ROLE SPECIAL INSTRUCTION

Customer Role ID (FK)
Role Special Instruction ID

Role Special Instruction Description
Role Special Instruction From Date
Role Special Instruction To Date

CUSTOMER RELATED

Customer ID (FK)
Customer Role ID (FK)
Customer Related ID (FK)
Customer Related Role Code (FK)
Customer Related Start Date

Customer Related End Date
Customer Structure Type (FK)
Customer Related Reason Code (FK)
Customer Related Status Type Code (FK)

CUSTOMER

Customer ID

Customer Description
Customer Start Date
Customer End Date
Customer Subtype Code (FK)
Customer Type Code (FK)
Customer Initial Data Source Type Code (FK)
GDPR/CCPA Eligible Y N
SEC Classification ID (FK)

STATUS

Status ID

Status Code
Status Description

CUSTOMER /STATUS

Customer ID (FK)
Customer Status ID (FK)
Customer Status Start Date

Customer Status End Date
Customer Status Code
Customer Status Reason Code (FK)

HOUSEHOLD

Household ID (FK)

Household Title
Household Count
Household Child Count
Household Financial Manager Name
Household Financial Manager Employer
Household Financial Goal 1
Household Financial Goal 2
Household Financial Goal 3
Auto Support Payment Monthly
Auto Support Individual Name

SEC CLASSIFICATION

SEC Classification ID

SEC Classification Education Code (FK)
SEC Classification Employer
SEC Classification Occupation Code (FK)

HOUSEHOLD MEMBER

Household ID (FK)
Individual ID (FK)
Householdl Member Datetime

Household Member Type Code
Household Member Type Description

INDIVIDUAL NAME

Individual ID (FK)

First Name
Middle Name 1
Middle Name 2
Family Name
Suffix
Nickname
Maiden Name
Alternate Name
Individual Full Name

CUSTOMER FINANCIAL DOCUMENT/ KYC

Customer ID (FK)
Financial Document Start Date
Customer Document Type Id (FK)
Data Source Type Code (FK)

Financial Document End Date
Financial Document Id (FK)
Financial Document Time Period Code (FK)

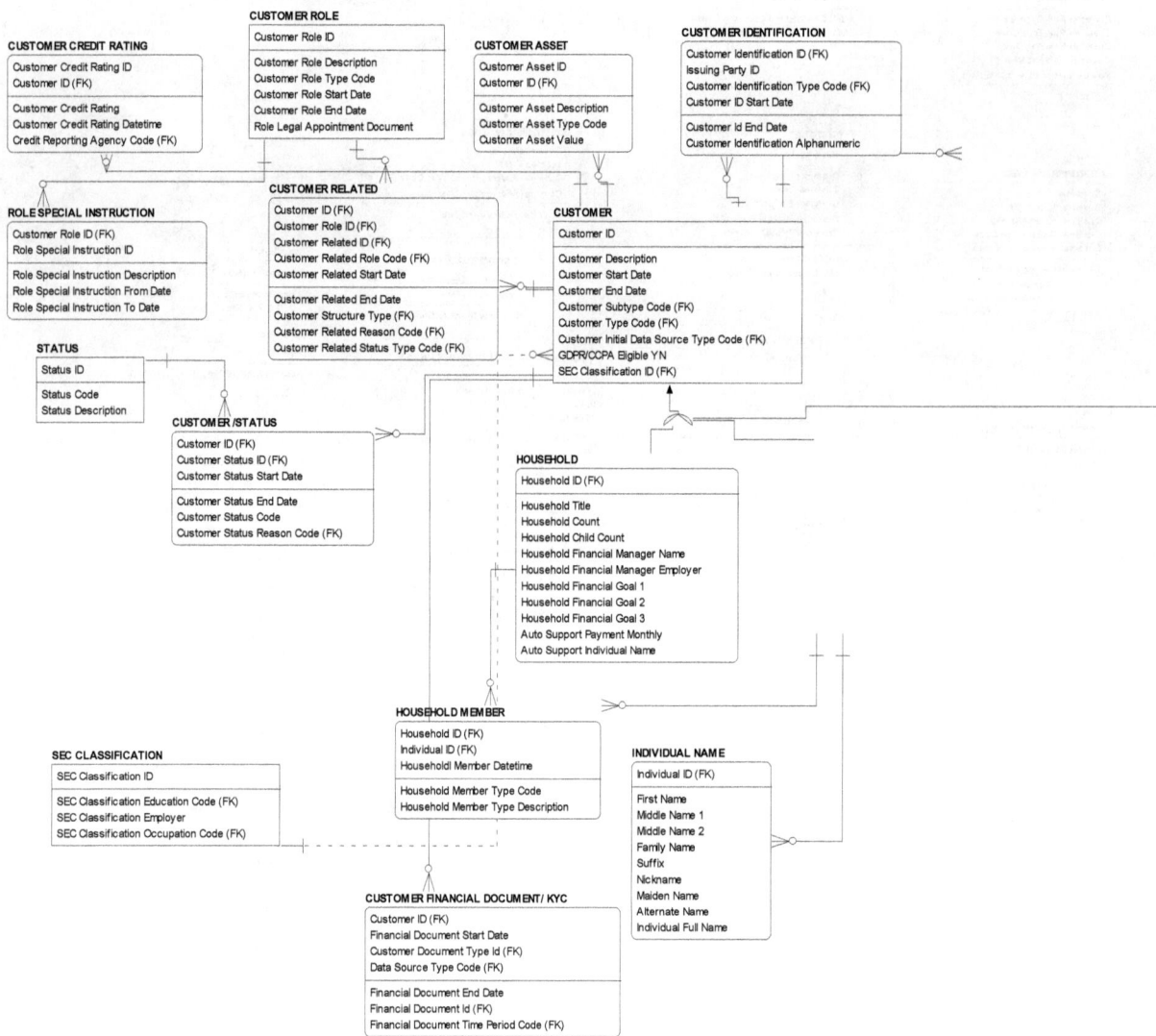

Model 7.01 Customer, left side of the model

CUSTOMER SALUTATION
Customer Salutation ID
Customer ID (FK)

Customer Salutation Code

LOCATION
Location ID

Location Subtype Code (FK)

TIME ZONE
Location ID (FK)

Time Zone Name
UTC Official Time

CUSTOMER/LOCATION
Customer ID (FK)
Location ID (FK)
Customer Address Usage Type Code (FK)
Customer Address Start Date

Customer Address End Date

ORGANIZATION
Organization ID (FK)

Organization Legal Name
Organization Short Name
Organization Purpose
Organization Type Code FK)
Organization Subtype Code (FK)
Organization Established Date
Organization Closed Date
Parent Organization ID (FK)
Legal Classification Code (FK)
Ownership Type Code (FK)
DUNS ID
BIC Business Code (FK)
NAICS Sumber
Organization Fiscal Month Number
Organization Fiscal Day Number
Basel Organization Type Code (FK)
Basel Market Participant Code (FK)
Basel Eligible Central Indicator YN
Basel Business Code (FK)

ADDRESS
Address ID (FK)

Address Subtype Code (FK)

STREET ADDRESS
Street Address ID (FK)

Address Line 1 Text
Address Line 2 Text
Address Line 3 Text
Dwelling Type Code (FK)
City Name
State Name
Country ID (FK)
Territory Name
Postal Code ID (FK)
Carrier Route Text

INDIVIDUAL
Individual ID (FK)

Birth Date
Death Date
Gender Type Code (FK)
Tax Bracket Code (FK)
VIP Type Code (FK)
Employment Start Date
Retirement Date
Primary Account Administrator YN
Account Decision Maker YN

INTERNAL ORGANIZATION
Internal Organization ID (FK)

Internal Organization Type Code
Internal Organization Subtype Code
Internal Organization Number

TELEPHINE NUMBER
Telephone Number ID (FK) (FK)

Area Code
Exchange Number
Line Number
Extension Number

OVERSEAS MILITARY ADDRESS
Overseas Military Address ID (FK)

Overseas Military Postal Code ID (FK)
Overseas Military City ID (FK)
Overseas Military Territory ID (FK)

ELECTRONIC ADDRESS
Electronic Address ID (FK)

Electronic Address Subtype Code (FK)
Electronic Address Text
Electronic Address Domain Name
Domain Root Code (FK)

BUSINESS
Business ID (FK)

Business Legal Start Date
Business Legal End Date
Stock Exchange Listed Ind YN
Business Category Code (FK)
Tax Bracket Code (FK)

POST OFFICE BOX ADDRESS
Post Office Box ID (FK)

Post Office Box Number
City ID (FK)
Country ID (FK)
Postal Code ID (FK)
Territory ID (FK)

INTERNET PROTOCOL ADDRESS
Electromnic Address ID (FK)
Internet Protocol Address ID

Internet Protocol Address Number
Internet Protocol Address ID (FK)
Internet Protocol Address Registered by Party ID (FK)
Internet Protocol Network Name

FINANCIAL INSTITUTION
Financial Institution ID (FK)

Financial Institution Type Code (FK)
Financial Institution Industry Assigned Number

ASSOCIATION
Association ID (FK)

Association Type Code
Association Type Description

GOVERNMENT
Government ID (FK)

Government Unit Type Code
Government Unit Description

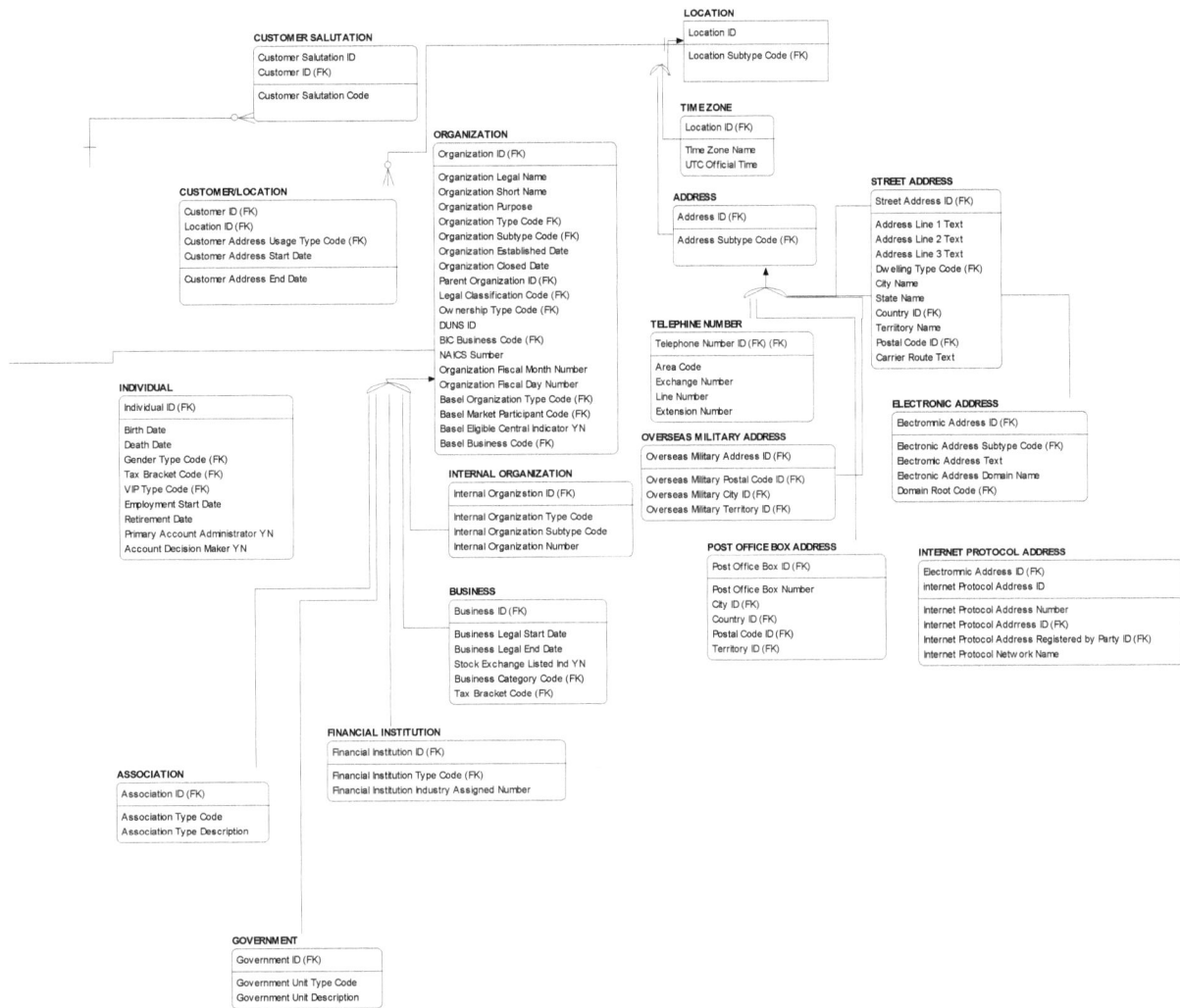

Model 7.02 Customer, right side of the model

When you see an attribute in the key of the entity or listed as an attribute with an (FK), and you do not see its source entity, that is because the source entity was left out on purpose for space reasons and it usually is a set of code values unique to the Firm. OR, the FK is the subtype of the entity itself and the child or children are diagrammed underneath the parent entity.

Many old-fashioned databases have attributes that collect data about race, religion, ethnicity, and nationality. If your business is doing this or plans to do this, it better have a good reason for doing so, and it must be easily explainable to regulators, your HR department, and the court! Try to categorize people only to the extent that your business requires it and not from habit. Note that the Gender attribute is left in the Individual entity since many businesses do sell gender-specific products.

Now for the entity 'Location,' which can be a subject area unto itself. In the Customer Logical model, the 'Location' entity was hanging off the right side of the model, with a relationship to its resolution entity 'Customer/Location.'

LOCATION

Location ID
Location Subtype Code (FK)

TIME ZONE

Location ID (FK)
Time Zone Name
UTC Official Time

ADDRESS

Address ID (FK)
Address Subtype Code (FK)

STREET ADDRESS

Street Address ID (FK)
Address Line 1 Text
Address Line 2 Text
Address Line 3 Text
Dwelling Type Code (FK)
City Name
State Name
Country ID (FK)
Territory Name
Postal Code ID (FK)
Carrier Route Text

TELEPHINE NUMBER

Telephone Number ID (FK) (FK)
Area Code
Exchange Number
Line Number
Extension Number

ELECTRONIC ADDRESS

Electromnic Address ID (FK)
Electronic Address Subtype Code (FK)
Electronic Address Text
Electronic Address Domain Name
Domain Root Code (FK)

OVERSEAS MILITARY ADDRESS

Overseas Military Address ID (FK)
Overseas Military Postal Code ID (FK)
Overseas Military City ID (FK)
Overseas Military Territory ID (FK)

POST OFFICE BOX ADDRESS

Post Office Box ID (FK)
Post Office Box Number
City ID (FK)
Country ID (FK)
Postal Code ID (FK)
Territory ID (FK)

INTERNET PROTOCOL ADDRESS

Electromnic Address ID (FK)
internet Protocol Address ID
Internet Protocol Address Number
Internet Protocol Addrress ID (FK)
Internet Protocol Address Registered by Party ID (FK)
Internet Protocol Network Name

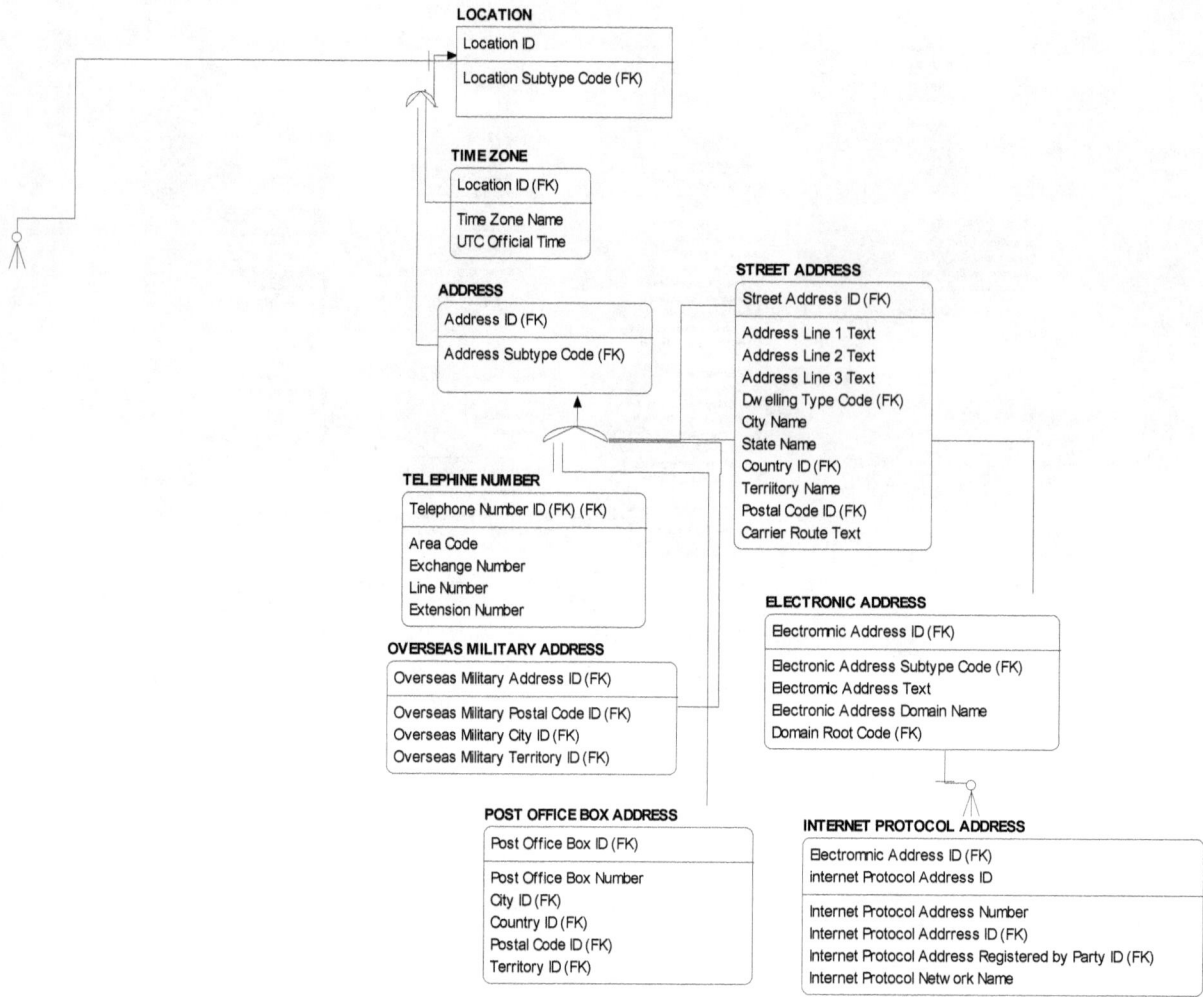

Model 7.03 Location Logical model

Product Logical Models

A Generic Product Logical ERD

Without specifying a particular Financial Industry instrument, here is a (rather high-level) Logical Product model:

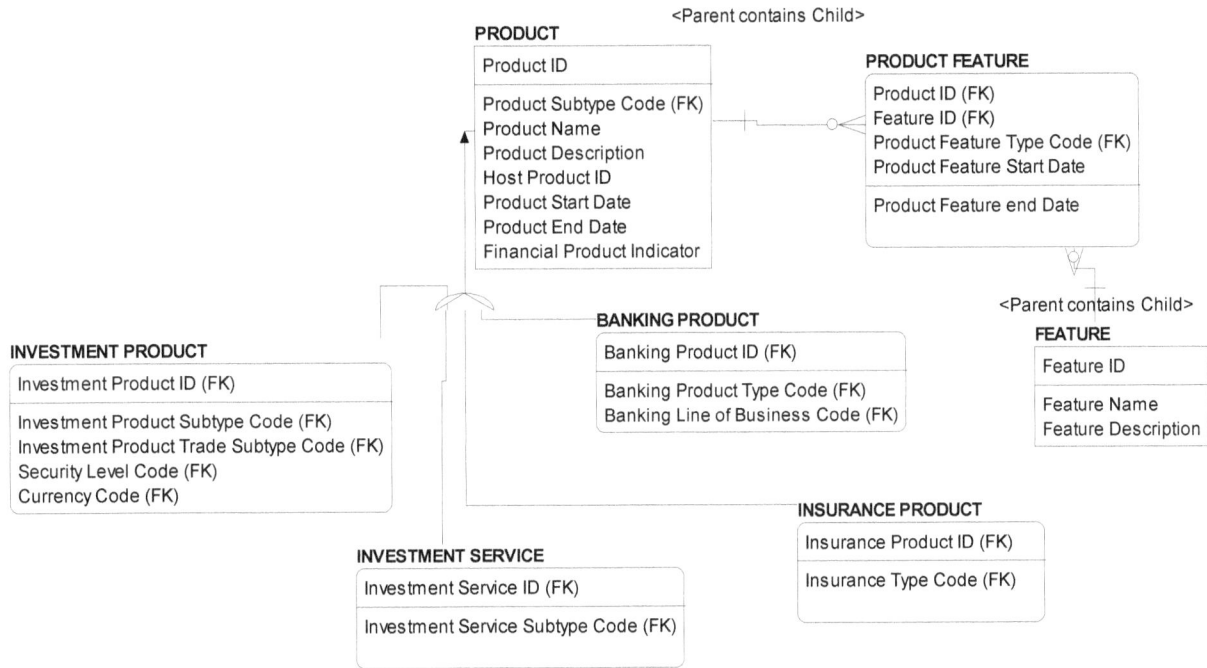

Model 7.5 High-level Product Logical ERD

Customer and Product subject areas (i.e., these "starter models") actually become your 'masterfiles' or master subject areas of the Logical and Physical models. Enhance, expand, and/or modify them according to the requirements of your business.

In a large organization, it can help to have permanent staff assigned to maintain the integrity of Customer and Product data in these files. It doesn't have to be a large staff–just enough to apply data governance rules and practices. While loading into the database, examining each data set for accuracy is extremely helpful. Some of this can be automated, but there must always be a human to ensure the automation does not miss anything.

Don't forget to schedule and conduct periodic model reviews as the modeling work progresses. Reviews and discussions with stakeholders/users can provide additional insight–even if they just agree and sign off. Always issue meeting minutes and invite senior management and/or their proxies to model reviews.

After the above sections on Customer and Product, and to save on model space, Customer and Product will be represented in ERDs as small empty boxes. Now you know what they really are!

FOUR

The Logical Model Templates

The Logical Model Templates are:

- Retail and Commercial Banking
- Credit Cards
- Securities, Investments, and Brokerage
- Property, Casualty and Life Insurance
- Capital and Finance

A complete Logical data model includes all of the relevant entities and attributes–fully defined. Note that there are plenty of industry-standard definitions – from Investopedia.com to SEC.gov to https://content.naic.org. If attributes arise from regulations or security concerns, state the rule or concern, its associated reference number, and the sentence(s) from the regulation for the sake of the developers and users.

Your own business definitions should coincide, more or less, with industry-standard definitions. **If they do not, find out why.** Perhaps your in-house terminology needs to change. You will not get the industry to change unless you are the Chairperson of the Federal Reserve. If your business uses a phrase (e.g., Fixed Income LEAPS) and its definition inside your Firm is substantially different from the industry's definition, you have two alternatives: (a) Write this up, not only in your model definitions, but also in Interoffice Documentation or (b) design a different term to denote your in-house definition.

In addition to entities and attributes, the Logical model must show the relationships between entities, suggested data types, and data lengths. Data types may be the best experience of the Modeler, or they may have been cast in stone by the data source. There are always trade-offs. For example, you may recognize the need for five lines of address for international mail. However, if your source system provides only three lines, your options are (a) adapt to three lines, (b) get your source system to expand its address space, (c) create a new entity for the purpose of storing the extra lines of address, or (d) transform the data prior to loading into the database. Be sure to convey this to your developers using whatever method you choose.

Eh bien, we begin Logical modeling.

Retail Banking

The subsequent Logical ERDs address Retail Banking. Retail Banking provides agreements and their subsequent accounts for Checking, Savings, Mortgages, Home Equity Loans, Personal Loans, and CDs. Retail banks could provide other services, but since this is a starter template, we will not go into every single service provided by small, mid-sized, or major banks. We will address credit cards separately.

A Logical data model takes each entity in a Conceptual model and details it as a subject area, consisting of lower level/refined entities and attributes.

Agreement is the contract between a Customer and a Bank which specifies:

- which services are to be made available to the Customer, and

- how the Agreement can be modified or terminated, depending on the Bank's rules (and State/Federal regulations).

Accounts, such as savings, checking, and loan accounts, are authorized by the Agreement.

The Account (as seen on a potential Statement) contains Line Items; a Line Item is the result of an Event. An Event, such as a deposit, payment, or withdrawal, is created by either the Customer or the Bank.

Let's do a model review of a Retail Banking activity: depositing a check. Until just a few years ago, you walked the check into your bank and up to a teller's window to hand it over for deposit. Now, you can just take a picture of the check and email or wire it into your account. We'll just start with the event:

- **Event**–Deposit a check. The activity of depositing a check must be a code in the entity Event. Whether it is just an attribute code or a subtype code is up to you, your business requirement, and your design.

- **Bank**–Submits the check data to a 3rd party for validation or does the validation in-house by reaching out for Customer information. The system must recognize that the Customer is a valid Customer, and that they have an Account (associated with an Agreement) which can accept a check deposit. Also, the check data must be good, and there must be internal security inspection(s) for this. The Bank confirms that the check is good, or returns it if it is not good. Let's assume the check is good.

- **Account**–Records the date of deposit, amount, and description associated with a checking deposit. Credits the Account with deposited funds.

- **Line Item**–Prints or displays a receipt for you. A bit of discussion about Line Item here. Imagine your account statement has a line item for each event of a deposit, withdrawal, interest, or fee. The entity Line Item supplies the Line Item Number. However, we get the details of the Line Item's description and price from the entity Product Feature. Product Feature has a complete subtype cluster containing entities for Date Feature, Description Feature, and Amount Feature.

On the next page (32) we find the entire Logical data model, 8.0, required to support checking within Retail Banking. Page 33 displays the left side of the data model in a larger font and page 34 displays the right side of the data model.

CUSTOMER
Customer ID

CUSTOMER/EVENT
Customer ID (FK)
Event ID (FK)

Customer Event Type (FK)
Customer Event Subtype (FK)

EVENT
Event ID

Event Start Datetime
Event End Datetime

FINANCIAL EVENT
Event ID (FK)

financial Event Type (FK)

CUSTOMER/PRODUCT
Customer ID (FK)
Product ID (FK)

PRODUCT
Product ID

Product Subtype Code (FK)
Product Description
Product Name
Host Product ID
Product Start Date
Product End Date
Financial Product Indicator YN
Product Creation Date
Product Text

PRODUCT/FEATURE
Feature ID (FK)
Product ID (FK)
Product Feature type Code (FK)
Product Feature Start Date

Product Feature End Date

FEATURE
Feature ID

Feature Subtype Code (FK)
Feature Name
Feature Description
Feature Classification ID (FK)

AGREEMENT
Agreement ID

Agreement Type (FK)
Agreement Subtype (FK)
Agreement Start Date
Agreement End Date
Agreement Risk Code (FK)
Agreement Currency Code (FK)

INVESTMENT PRODUCT
Investment Product ID (FK)

Investment Product Trade Subtype Code (FK)
Investment Product Subtype Code (FK)
Currency Code (FK)
Day Count Basis Code (FK)
Seniority Level Code (FK)

TERM FEATURE
Feature ID (FK)

From Time Period Code (FK)
To Time Period Code (FK)
Until Age Code (FK)
From Time Period Number
To Time Period Number
Until Age Number

DATE FEATURE
Feature ID (FK)

Feature Datetime
Date Feature Due Day of Month

INVESTMENT SERVICE
Investment Service Product ID (FK)

Investment Service Subtype Code (FK)

AMOUNT FEATURE
Feature ID (FK)

To Feature Amount
Amount Time Period Code (FK)
Amount Time Period Number
Currency Code (FK)
From Feature Amount

ACCOUNT
Agreement ID (FK)
Customer ID (FK)
Account Start Date
Account Type (FK)

Account Subtype (FK)
Account End Date
Account Routing Number
Account Number
Account Name
Account Payment or Deposit
Account Payment Datetime
Account Payment Day of Month
Interest Indicator Y/N
Interest Amount
Interest Paid Datetime
Overdraft Indicator Y/N
Maximum Amount of Overdraft

INSURANCE PRODUCT
Insurance Product ID (FK)

Insurance Type Code (FK)

QUANTITY FEATURE
Feature ID (FK)

Quantity Time Period Code (FK)
Quantity Unit Measure Code (FK)
Feature Quantity
Feature Time Period Number

BANKING PRODUCT
Banking Product ID (FK)

Banking Product Type Code (FK)
Banking Line of Business Code (FK)

DESCRIPTION FEATURE
Feature ID (FK)

Descriptive Feature Type Code (FK)
Feature Description

CERTIFICATE OF DEPOSIT
CDt ID (FK)

CD Term
CD Face Value
CD Interest Rate
CD Early Withdrawal Date
CD Total Priinciple plus Interest Paid
CD Penalty for Early Withdrawal
CD For the Benefit Of

RATE FEATURE
Feature ID (FK)

Rate Feature Type Code (FK)
Rate Time Period Number
Rate Time Period Code (FK)

LINE ITEM
Line Item ID

Line Item Number
Line Item Balance
Agreement ID (FK)
Customer ID (FK)
Account Start Date (FK)
Account Type (FK) (FK)

MORTGAGE or LOAN see above
Banking Product ID (FK)

OTHER INTEREST RATE
Feature ID (FK)

From Other Feature Rate
To Other Feature Rate

FIXED INTEREST RATE
Feature ID (FK)

Fixed Interest Rate

VARIABLE INTEREST RATE
Feature ID (FK)

Spread Rate
Interest Index Code (FK)
Upper Limit Rate
Lower Limit Rate

INTEREST INDEX
Interest Index Code

Interest Index Description
Interest Index Time Period Code (FK)
Inerest Index Time Period Number
Currency Code (FK)

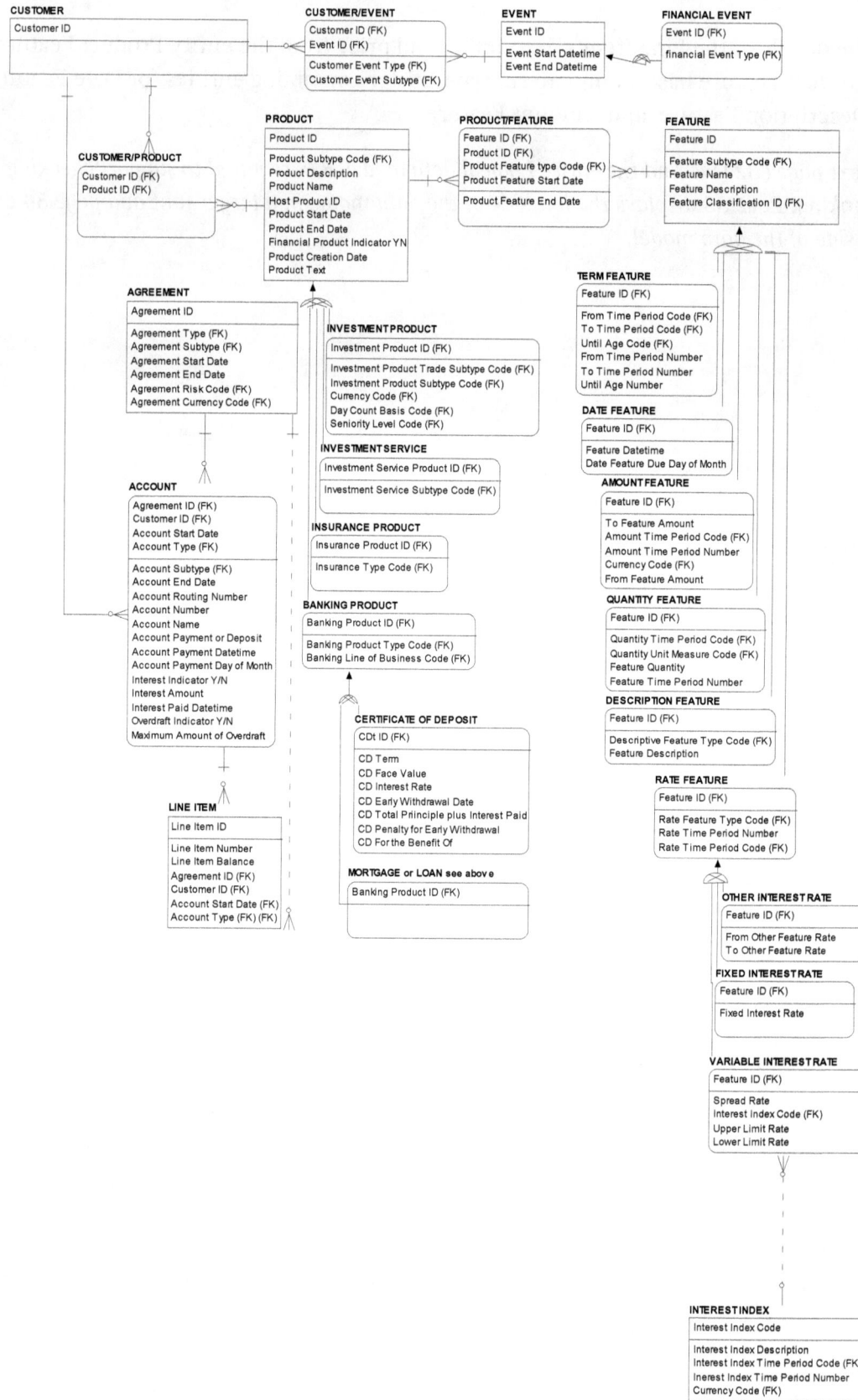

Model 8.0 Retail Banking Logical ERD

MORTGAGE/ LOAN

Mortgage Loan ID
Agreement ID (FK)
Mortgage Loan Type (FK)
Basic Mortgage Application Form
Basic Loan Application form
Required Doc for Mortgage Loan Application Code (FK)
Required Doc for Mortgage Loan Application Name
Required Doc for Mortgage Loan Application

<Parent contains Child>

CUSTOMER

Customer ID

<Parent contains Child>

<Parent contains Child>

<Parent contains Child>

CUSTOMER/PRODUCT

Customer ID (FK)
Product ID (FK)

AGREEMENT

Agreement ID
Agreement Type (FK)
Agreement Subtype (FK)
Agreement Start Date
Agreement End Date
Agreement Risk Code (FK)
Agreement Currency Code (FK)

<Parent contains Child>

ACCOUNT

Agreement ID (FK)
Customer ID (FK)
Account Start Date
Account Type (FK(
Account Subtype (FK)
Account End Date
Account Routing Number
Account Number
Account Name
Account Payment or Deposit
Account Payment Datetime
Account Payment Day of Month
Interest Indicator Y/N
Interest Paid Datetime
Interest Amount
Overdraft Indicator Y/N
Maximum Amount of Overdraft

LOAN COLLATERAL

Loan Collateral ID
Collateral Type Code (FK)
Collateral Item Text
Collateral Purpose Text
Collateral Value
Mortgage Loan ID (FK)
Customer ID (FK)

CUSTOMER/ MORTGAGE/ LOAN

Mortgage Loan ID (FK)
Customer ID (FK)
Property Address Code (FK)
Property Appraisal Date
Appraised Property Value
Mortgage Loan Amount
Mortgage Loan Borrow Date
Mortgage Loan End Date
Arrears Y/N
Collateralized Y/N
Comparable Property Address 1
Comparable Property Value 1
Comparable Property Address 2
Comparable Property Value 2
Loan Collateral ID (FK)

<Parent contains Child>

LINE ITEM

Line Item ID
Line Item Number
Line Item Balance
Agreement ID (FK)
Customer ID (FK)
Account Start Date (FK)
Account Type (FK((FK)

MORTGAGE LOAN ARREARS

Mortgage Loan Arrears ID
Mortgage Loan ID (FK)
Customer ID (FK)
Arrears Month Count
In Arrears Initial Date
Arrears Month Limit
Number of Arrears Occurances

BANKING PRODUCT

Banking Product ID (FK)
Banking Product Type Code (FK)
Banking Line of Business Code (FK)

EVENT

Event ID
Event Start Datetime
Event End Datetime

<Parent contains Child>

Z
<Parent contains Child>

MORTGAGE LOAN FORECLOSURE

Mortgage Loan Foreclosure ID
In Foreclosure Y/N
Foreclosure Notice Served Y/N
Foreclosure Notice Served Datetime
Mortgage Loan ID (FK)
Customer ID (FK)

MORTGAGE or LOAN see above

Mortgage/Loan ID (FK)

CERTIFICATE OF DEPOSIT

CDt ID (FK)
CD Term
CD Face Value
CD Interest Rate
CD Early Withdrawal Date
CD Total Priinciple plus Interest Paid
CD Penalty for Early Withdrawal
CD For the Benefit Of

<Parent contains Child>

PRE PAYMENT

Pre Payment ID
Mortgage Loan ID (FK)
Customer ID (FK)
Pre Payment Allowed Y/N
PrePayment Amount
Principle After Pre Payment
Pre Payment Datetime

FINANCIAL EVENT

Event ID (FK)
financial Event Type (FK)

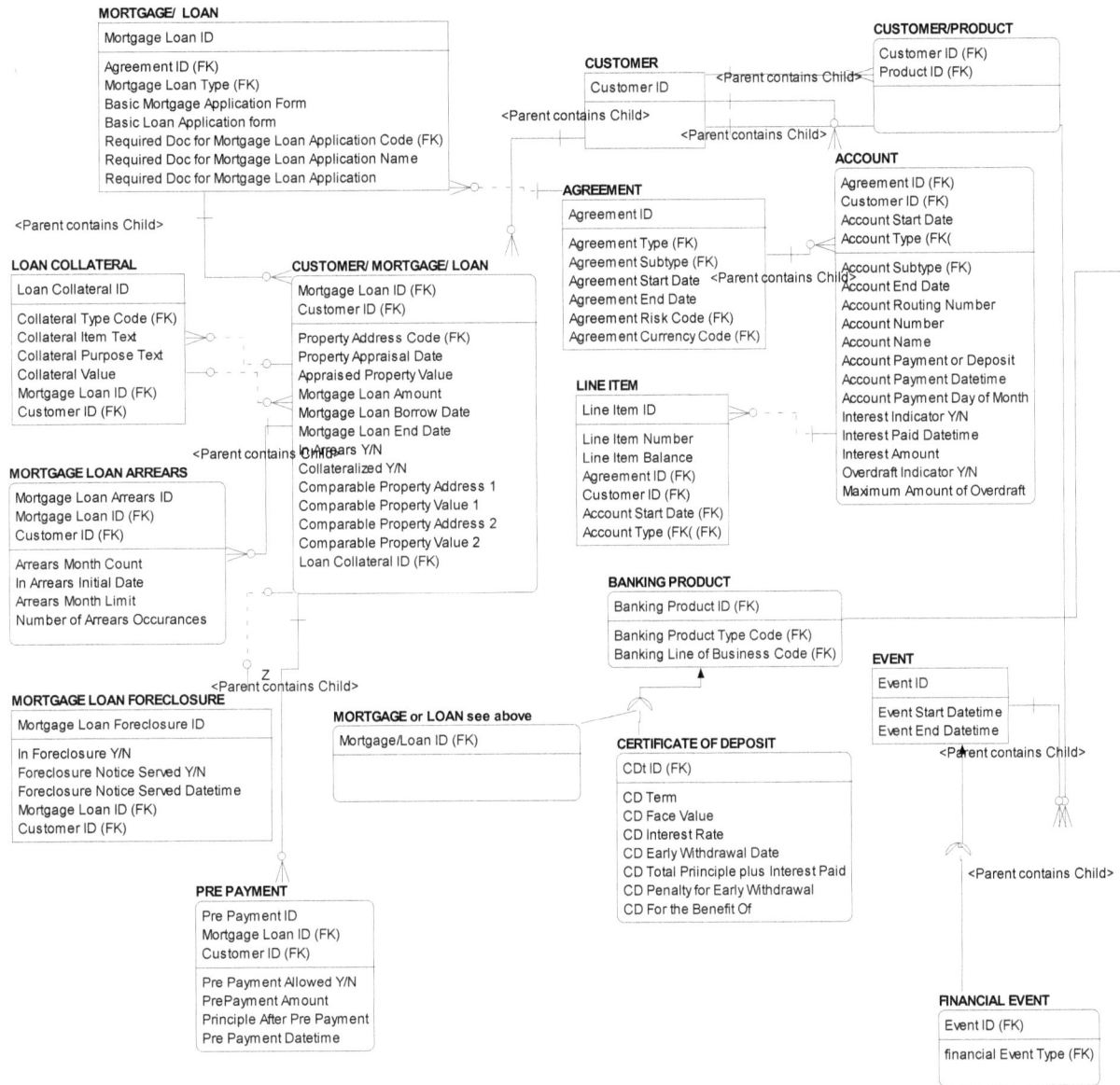

Model 8.01 Retail Banking (checking) the left side of the Logical ERD

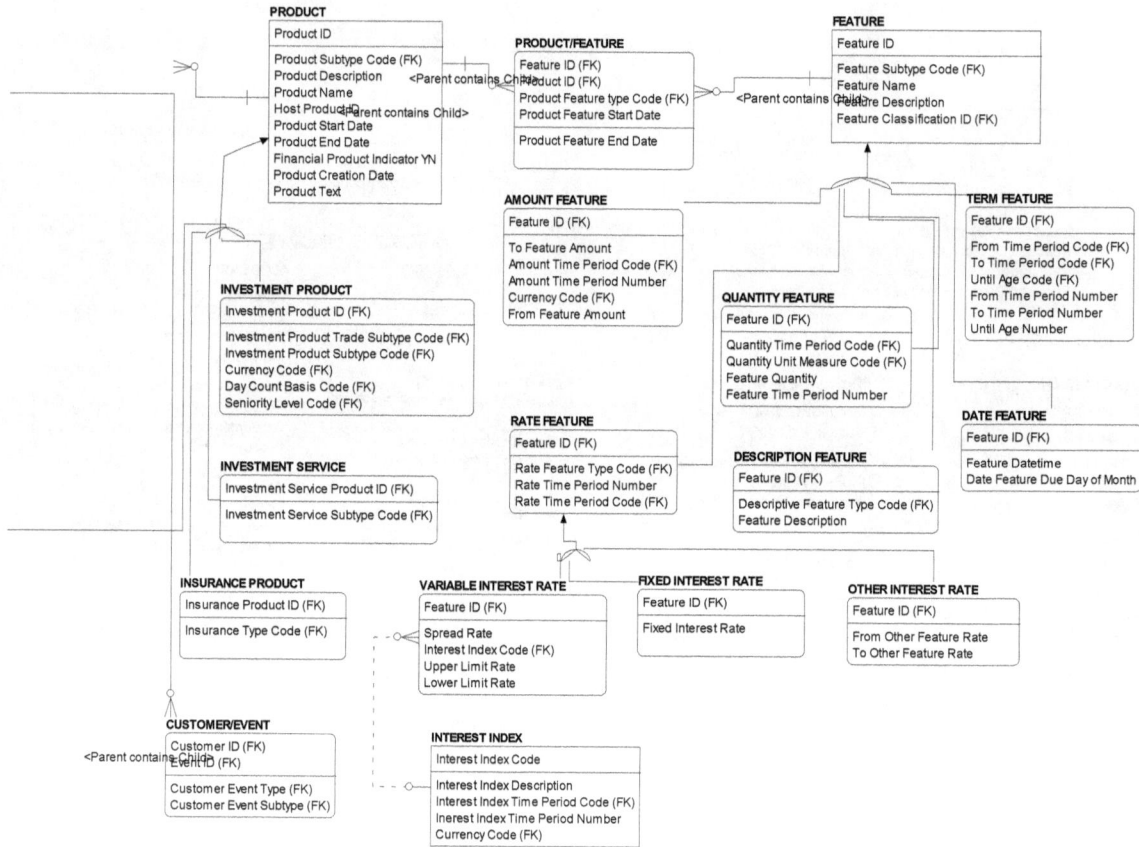

Model 8.02 Retail Banking (checking), right side of Logical ERD

Next, note that the information we need to support a Savings Account includes the following:

Type of Account   Account Number
Interest Percent   Interest Datetime
Interest Amount   Savings Balance
Deposit Amount   Deposit Datetime
Withdrawal Datetime   Withdrawal Amount

Savings Accounts are supported by the same logical model as Checking accounts, with the addition of two attributes, as follows:

Required Savings Account attributes	Mapped to Logical Checking ERD: Entity/Attribute	Added to Logical Checking ERD to make it include Savings
Type of Savings Account	Account/Account Type	
Savings Account Number	Account/Account Number	
% Interest Rate	Account/Interest Rate	
Interest paid to Savings Account		Account/Interest Amount
Interest paid to Savings Account on Date		Account/Interest Paid Datetime
Savings Account Balance	Line Item/Line Item Balance	

Required Savings Account attributes	Mapped to Logical Checking ERD: Entity/Attribute	Added to Logical Checking ERD to make it include Savings
Savings Deposit Amount	Amount Feature/To Feature Amount	
Savings Deposit Datetime	Event/Event End Datetime	
Savings Withdrawal Amount	Amount Feature/From Feature Amount	
Savings Withdrawal Datetime	Event/Event End Datetime	

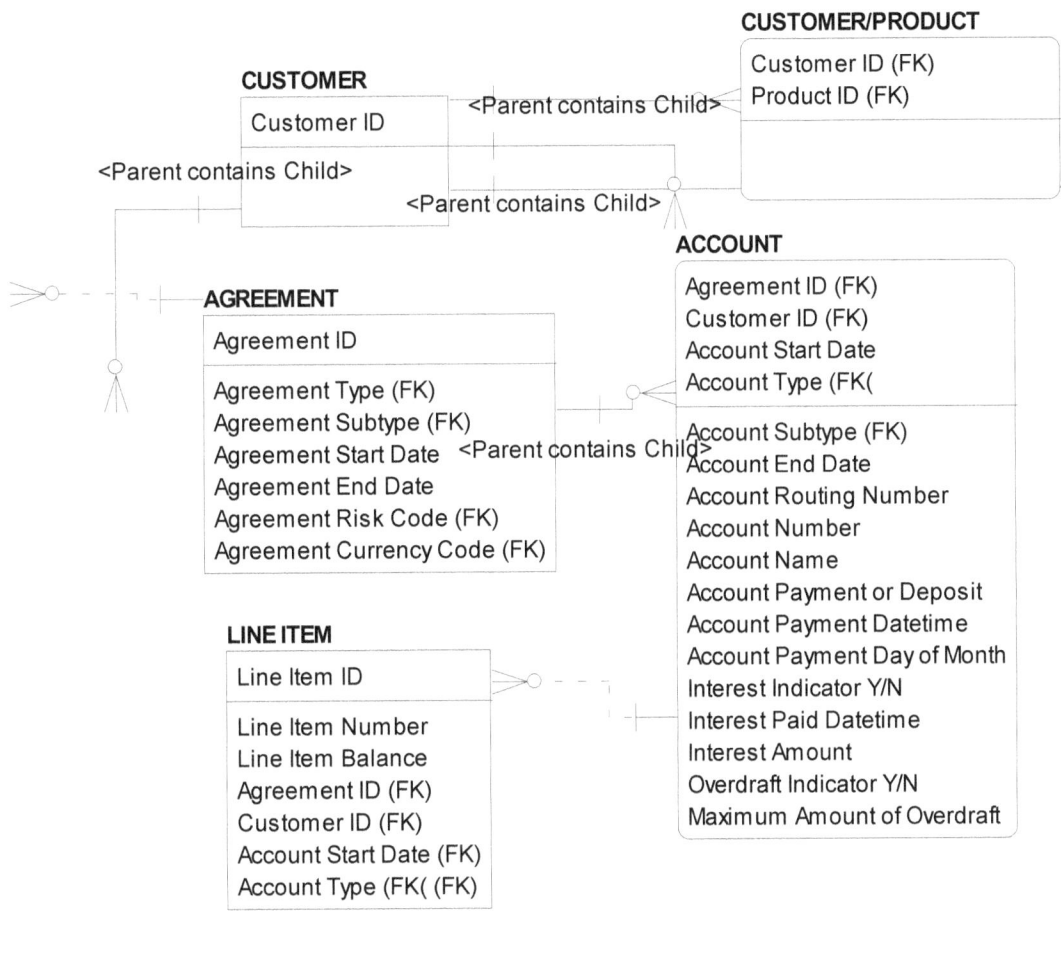

Model 8.03 Checking and Savings Accounts

So, now we have a basic Logical model that supports both Checking and Savings in a Retail Bank.

Mortgage

What about the application for a mortgage and the mortgage itself?

A mortgage or mortgage loan is the money a customer has borrowed from a lender for the purpose of purchasing or refinancing a home or property. If the customer does not make the agreed payments to the lender, the lender has the right to repossess the home or property.

Here is a starter set of attributes that support Mortgages:

A list of required documents for a mortgage application
Fixed or variable rate
Term of mortgage in years
Late fee incurred Day of Month
Late Fee Percentage
Pre-payment Amount
Pre-payment Datetime
Arrears Month Limit
Foreclosure Served Datetime
Date RE Appraised
Mortgage Payment

Basic mortgage application form
Amount borrowed
Payment Due Day of month
Late fee Amount
Pre-payment Allowed (Y/N)
Principle Balance After Pre-payment
Arrears Month Count
In Foreclosure (Y/N)
Value of Real Estate
Comparable Property 1,2,3
Date Mortgage Payment Made

Only four of these objects map into the previous model; most do not. The ones that do map are as follows (and two attributes were added):

Required Mortgage attributes	Maps to Entity/Attribute	Add to Checking/Savings ERD
Fixed or variable rate mortgage	Rate Feature/Rate Feature Type Code	
Term of mortgage	Term Feature/From Time Period Code and Term Feature/To Time Period Code	
Payment due day of month		Date Feature/Date Feature Due Day of Month
Mortgage Loan Payment	Account/Account Payment	
Mortgage Loan Payment Date	Account/Account Payment Date	
Type of Mortgage or Loan		Mortgage Loan Type (FK)

Four new entities need to be added to the previous model to support mortgages: Mortgage/Loan, Pre-Payment, Arrears, and Foreclosure:

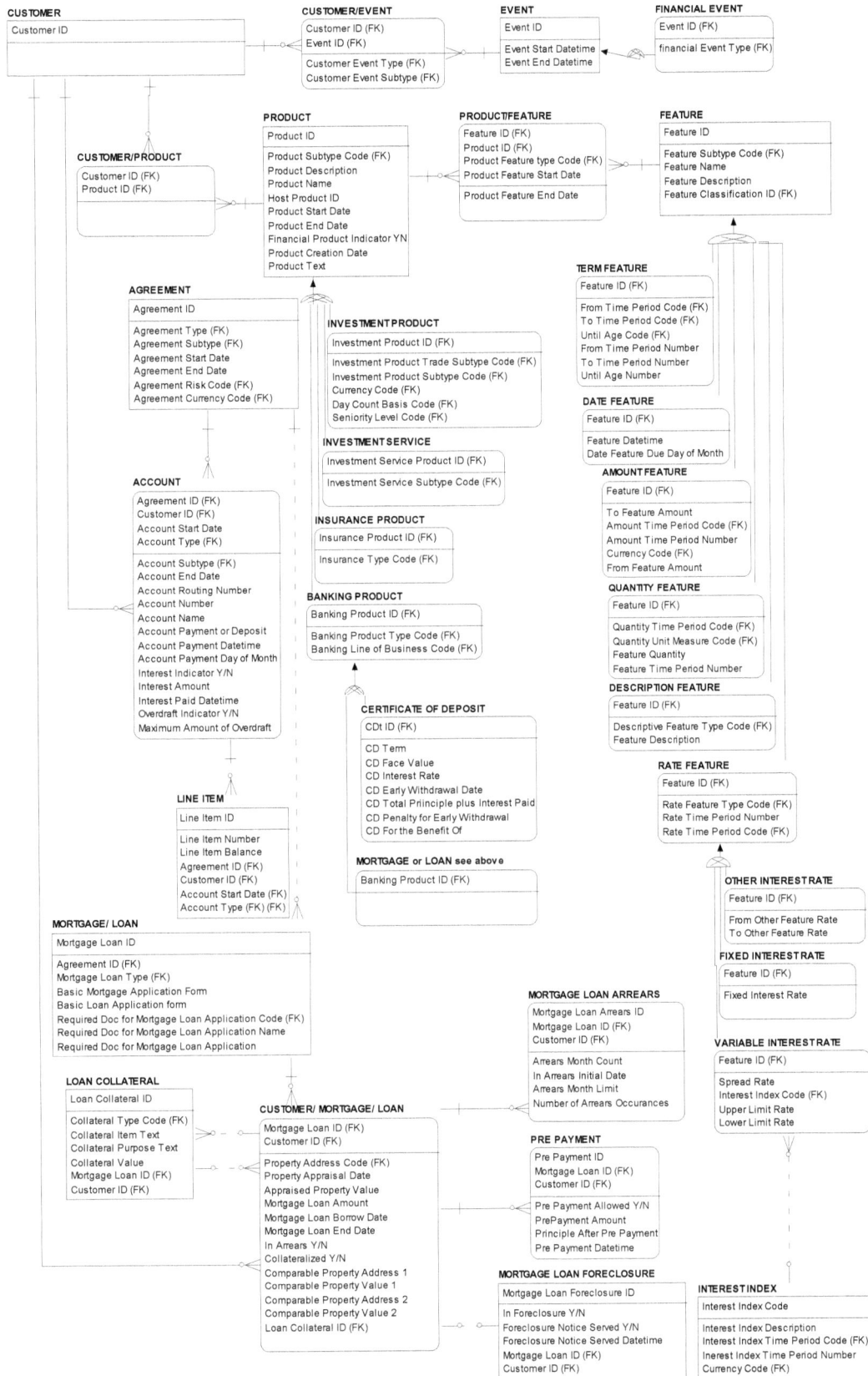

CUSTOMER
- Customer ID

CUSTOMER/EVENT
- Customer ID (FK)
- Event ID (FK)
- Customer Event Type (FK)
- Customer Event Subtype (FK)

EVENT
- Event ID
- Event Start Datetime
- Event End Datetime

FINANCIAL EVENT
- Event ID (FK)
- financial Event Type (FK)

CUSTOMER/PRODUCT
- Customer ID (FK)
- Product ID (FK)

PRODUCT
- Product ID
- Product Subtype Code (FK)
- Product Description
- Product Name
- Host Product ID
- Product Start Date
- Product End Date
- Financial Product Indicator YN
- Product Creation Date
- Product Text

PRODUCT/FEATURE
- Feature ID (FK)
- Product ID (FK)
- Product Feature type Code (FK)
- Product Feature Start Date
- Product Feature End Date

FEATURE
- Feature ID
- Feature Subtype Code (FK)
- Feature Name
- Feature Description
- Feature Classification ID (FK)

AGREEMENT
- Agreement ID
- Agreement Type (FK)
- Agreement Subtype (FK)
- Agreement Start Date
- Agreement End Date
- Agreement Risk Code (FK)
- Agreement Currency Code (FK)

INVESTMENT PRODUCT
- Investment Product ID (FK)
- Investment Product Trade Subtype Code (FK)
- Investment Product Subtype Code (FK)
- Currency Code (FK)
- Day Count Basis Code (FK)
- Seniority Level Code (FK)

TERM FEATURE
- Feature ID (FK)
- From Time Period Code (FK)
- To Time Period Code (FK)
- Until Age Code (FK)
- From Time Period Number
- To Time Period Number
- Until Age Number

DATE FEATURE
- Feature ID (FK)
- Feature Datetime
- Date Feature Due Day of Month

INVESTMENT SERVICE
- Investment Service Product ID (FK)
- Investment Service Subtype Code (FK)

ACCOUNT
- Agreement ID (FK)
- Customer ID (FK)
- Account Start Date
- Account Type (FK)
- Account Subtype (FK)
- Account End Date
- Account Routing Number
- Account Number
- Account Name
- Account Payment or Deposit
- Account Payment Datetime
- Account Payment Day of Month
- Interest Indicator Y/N
- Interest Amount
- Interest Paid Datetime
- Overdraft Indicator Y/N
- Maximum Amount of Overdraft

INSURANCE PRODUCT
- Insurance Product ID (FK)
- Insurance Type Code (FK)

AMOUNT FEATURE
- Feature ID (FK)
- To Feature Amount
- Amount Time Period Code (FK)
- Amount Time Period Number
- Currency Code (FK)
- From Feature Amount

QUANTITY FEATURE
- Feature ID (FK)
- Quantity Time Period Code (FK)
- Quantity Unit Measure Code (FK)
- Feature Quantity
- Feature Time Period Number

BANKING PRODUCT
- Banking Product ID (FK)
- Banking Product Type Code (FK)
- Banking Line of Business Code (FK)

DESCRIPTION FEATURE
- Feature ID (FK)
- Descriptive Feature Type Code (FK)
- Feature Description

CERTIFICATE OF DEPOSIT
- CDt ID (FK)
- CD Term
- CD Face Value
- CD Interest Rate
- CD Early Withdrawal Date
- CD Total Prinicple plus Interest Paid
- CD Penalty for Early Withdrawal
- CD For the Benefit Of

RATE FEATURE
- Feature ID (FK)
- Rate Feature Type Code (FK)
- Rate Time Period Number
- Rate Time Period Code (FK)

LINE ITEM
- Line Item ID
- Line Item Number
- Line Item Balance
- Agreement ID (FK)
- Customer ID (FK)
- Account Start Date (FK)
- Account Type (FK) (FK)

MORTGAGE or LOAN see above
- Banking Product ID (FK)

OTHER INTEREST RATE
- Feature ID (FK)
- From Other Feature Rate
- To Other Feature Rate

FIXED INTEREST RATE
- Feature ID (FK)
- Fixed Interest Rate

MORTGAGE/ LOAN
- Mortgage Loan ID
- Agreement ID (FK)
- Mortgage Loan Type (FK)
- Basic Mortgage Application Form
- Basic Loan Application form
- Required Doc for Mortgage Loan Application Code (FK)
- Required Doc for Mortgage Loan Application Name
- Required Doc for Mortgage Loan Application

MORTGAGE LOAN ARREARS
- Mortgage Loan Arrears ID
- Mortgage Loan ID (FK)
- Customer ID (FK)
- Arrears Month Count
- In Arrears Initial Date
- Arrears Month Limit
- Number of Arrears Occurances

VARIABLE INTEREST RATE
- Feature ID (FK)
- Spread Rate
- Interest Index Code (FK)
- Upper Limit Rate
- Lower Limit Rate

LOAN COLLATERAL
- Loan Collateral ID
- Collateral Type Code (FK)
- Collateral Item Text
- Collateral Purpose Text
- Collateral Value
- Mortgage Loan ID (FK)
- Customer ID (FK)

CUSTOMER/ MORTGAGE/ LOAN
- Mortgage Loan ID (FK)
- Customer ID (FK)
- Property Address Code (FK)
- Property Appraisal Date
- Appraised Property Value
- Mortgage Loan Amount
- Mortgage Loan Borrow Date
- Mortgage Loan End Date
- In Arrears Y/N
- Collateralized Y/N
- Comparable Property Address 1
- Comparable Property Value 1
- Comparable Property Address 2
- Comparable Property Value 2
- Loan Collateral ID (FK)

PRE PAYMENT
- Pre Payment ID
- Mortgage Loan ID (FK)
- Customer ID (FK)
- Pre Payment Allowed Y/N
- PrePayment Amount
- Principle After Pre Payment
- Pre Payment Datetime

MORTGAGE LOAN FORECLOSURE
- Mortgage Loan Foreclosure ID
- In Foreclosure Y/N
- Foreclosure Notice Served Y/N
- Foreclosure Notice Served Datetime
- Mortgage Loan ID (FK)
- Customer ID (FK)

INTEREST INDEX
- Interest Index Code
- Interest Index Description
- Interest Index Time Period Code (FK)
- Inerest Index Time Period Number
- Currency Code (FK)

Model 8.5 Mortgage High Level Logical Data Model

A closer look at the new entities added to support Mortgages:

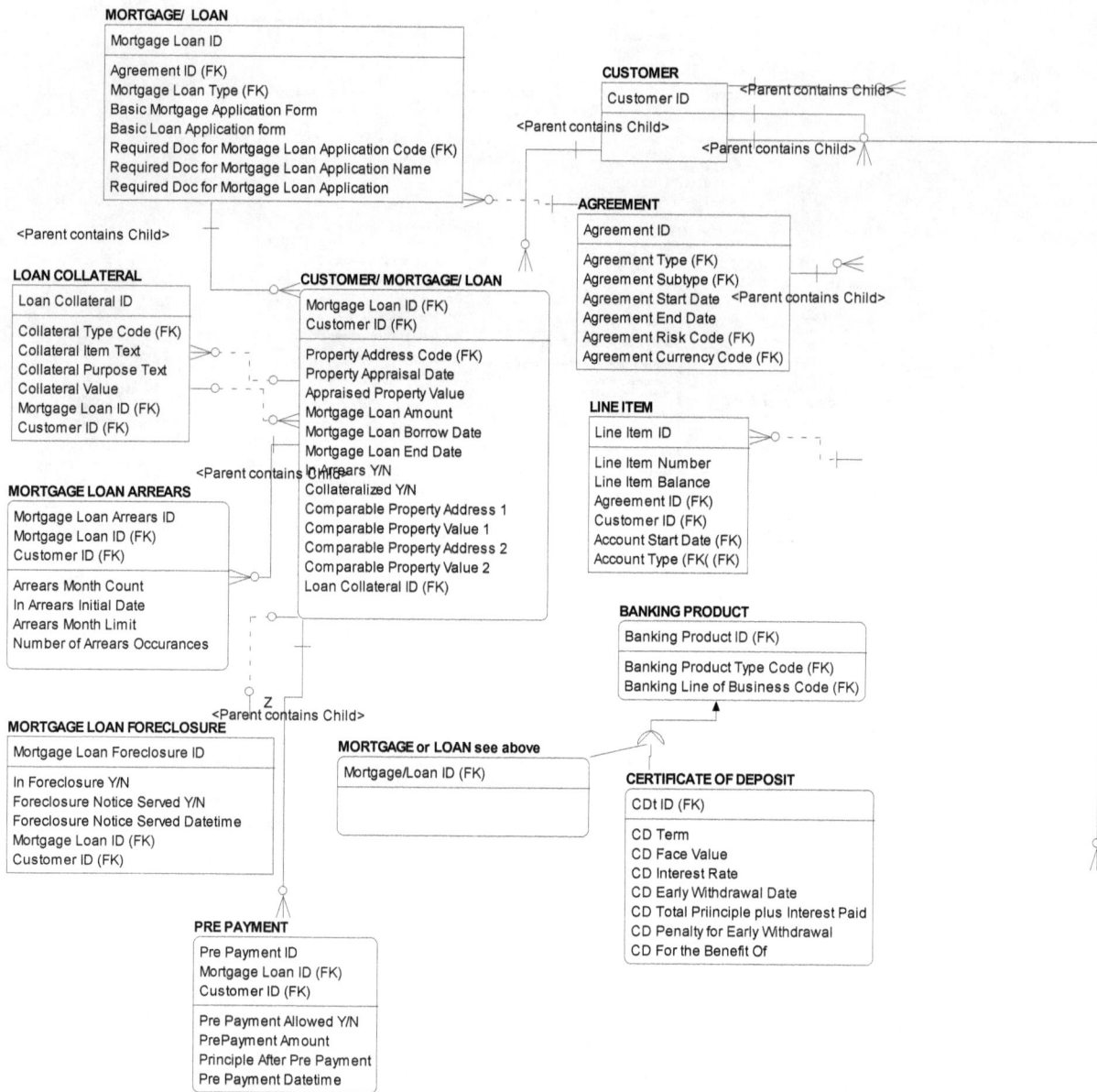

MORTGAGE/ LOAN

Mortgage Loan ID

Agreement ID (FK)
Mortgage Loan Type (FK)
Basic Mortgage Application Form
Basic Loan Application form
Required Doc for Mortgage Loan Application Code (FK)
Required Doc for Mortgage Loan Application Name
Required Doc for Mortgage Loan Application

<Parent contains Child>

CUSTOMER

Customer ID

<Parent contains Child>
<Parent contains Child>
<Parent contains Child>

AGREEMENT

Agreement ID

Agreement Type (FK)
Agreement Subtype (FK)
Agreement Start Date   <Parent contains Child>
Agreement End Date
Agreement Risk Code (FK)
Agreement Currency Code (FK)

LOAN COLLATERAL

Loan Collateral ID

Collateral Type Code (FK)
Collateral Item Text
Collateral Purpose Text
Collateral Value
Mortgage Loan ID (FK)
Customer ID (FK)

CUSTOMER/ MORTGAGE/ LOAN

Mortgage Loan ID (FK)
Customer ID (FK)

Property Address Code (FK)
Property Appraisal Date
Appraised Property Value
Mortgage Loan Amount
Mortgage Loan Borrow Date
Mortgage Loan End Date
In Arrears Y/N
Collateralized Y/N
Comparable Property Address 1
Comparable Property Value 1
Comparable Property Address 2
Comparable Property Value 2
Loan Collateral ID (FK)

<Parent contains Child>

LINE ITEM

Line Item ID

Line Item Number
Line Item Balance
Agreement ID (FK)
Customer ID (FK)
Account Start Date (FK)
Account Type (FK((FK)

MORTGAGE LOAN ARREARS

Mortgage Loan Arrears ID
Mortgage Loan ID (FK)
Customer ID (FK)

Arrears Month Count
In Arrears Initial Date
Arrears Month Limit
Number of Arrears Occurances

BANKING PRODUCT

Banking Product ID (FK)

Banking Product Type Code (FK)
Banking Line of Business Code (FK)

Z
<Parent contains Child>

MORTGAGE LOAN FORECLOSURE

Mortgage Loan Foreclosure ID

In Foreclosure Y/N
Foreclosure Notice Served Y/N
Foreclosure Notice Served Datetime
Mortgage Loan ID (FK)
Customer ID (FK)

MORTGAGE or LOAN see above

Mortgage/Loan ID (FK)

CERTIFICATE OF DEPOSIT

CDt ID (FK)

CD Term
CD Face Value
CD Interest Rate
CD Early Withdrawal Date
CD Total Priinciple plus Interest Paid
CD Penalty for Early Withdrawal
CD For the Benefit Of

PRE PAYMENT

Pre Payment ID
Mortgage Loan ID (FK)
Customer ID (FK)

Pre Payment Allowed Y/N
PrePayment Amount
Principle After Pre Payment
Pre Payment Datetime

Model 8.5.01 Mortgage Detail LDM

Home Equity Loan

A Home Equity Loan – application and maintenance - uses the same attributes as a Mortgage. The only difference is that you need an attribute in the entity Agreement to specify the Loan's Purpose. To see the Logical derivation of the Home Equity Line of Credit Agreement from the entity Agreement, refer back to the credit card model. Opposite the entity Credit Card you will see the Home Equity Line of Credit Agreement.

Personal and Business Loans

To support a Personal or a Business Loan, the following attributes are utilized, at a minimum:

- Borrower Credit Rating
- Loan Interest Rate
- Collateralized (Y/N)
- Collateral Value
- Loan End Date Loan
- In Arrears (Y/N)
- Number of Arrears Occurrences

Loan Amount
Loan Term
Collateral Item
Loan Start Date
Payment Day of Month
Number of Days in Arrears

CUSTOMER CREDIT RATING

Customer Credit Rating ID
Customer ID (FK)

Customer Credit Rating
Customer Credit Rating Datetime
Credit Reporting Agency Code (FK)

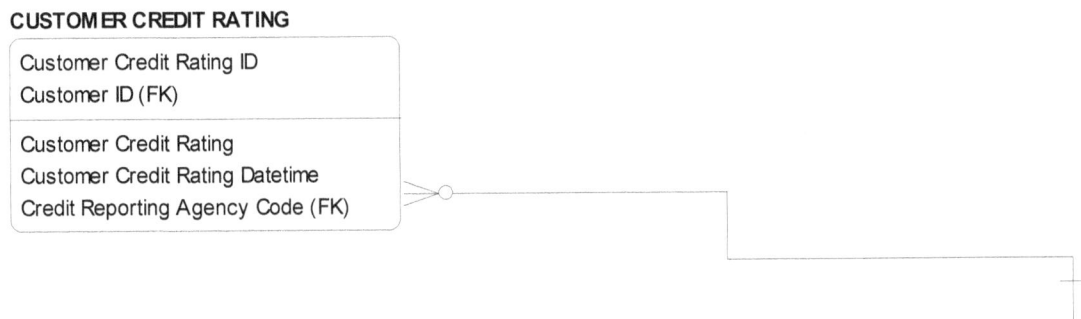

Model 9.0 Additional entity for Personal and Business Loans.

To support Personal Loans, we added the entity Customer Credit Rating to the Customer subject area. It has a one-to-many relationship from entity Customer to entity Customer Credit Rating. Note that this entity is not restricted to individuals but can also be used to check the credit rating of businesses and associations.

The Personal and Business Loan attributes listed above are either added to the current Logical data model if they are dependent upon the key of the entity or new entities have been created for them:

Necessary attribute	Added to existing entity	New entity added to Logical ERD
Borrower Credit Rating		Entity Customer Credit Rating Added to the Customer Subject Area
Loan Amount	Customer/Mortgage/Loan: Mortgage Loan Amount	
Loan Interest Rate	Rate Feature/use Variable or fixed entity	
Loan Term	Term Feature/From Time Interval Code and Term Feature/To Time Interval Code	
Collateralized Y/N	Customer/Mortgage/Loan: Collateralized Y/N	
Collateral Item		Entity Loan Collateral added. Loan Collateral/Collateral Item Text
Collateral Value		Loan Collateral/Collateral Value
Collateral Type Code		Loan Collateral/Collateral Type Code (FK)
Collateral Purpose Text		Loan Collateral/Collateral Purpose Text
Loan Start Date	Agreement/Start Date	
Loan End Date	Agreement/End Date	
Loan Payment Day of Month		Added to Account/Account Payment Day of Month
In Arrears Y/N	Customer/Mortgage/Loan: In Arrears Y/N	
In Arrears Date	Mortgage Loan Arrears/In Arrears Initial Date	
Number of Arrears Occurrences	Mortgage Loan Arrears./Number of Arrears Occurrences	

Model 9.01 Collateral entities added to support Loans – The ERD is on the next page.

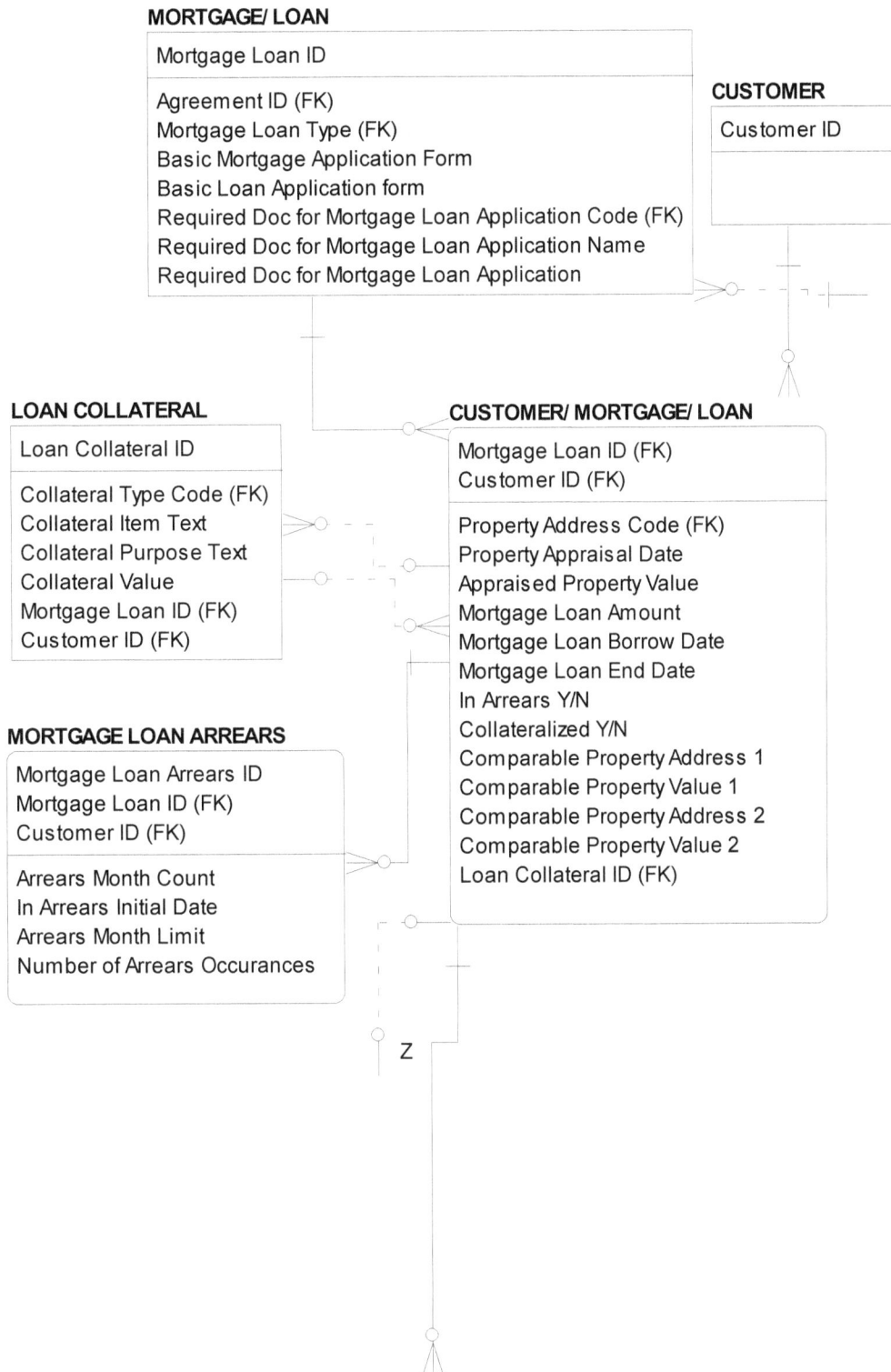

MORTGAGE/ LOAN

Mortgage Loan ID
Agreement ID (FK) Mortgage Loan Type (FK) Basic Mortgage Application Form Basic Loan Application form Required Doc for Mortgage Loan Application Code (FK) Required Doc for Mortgage Loan Application Name Required Doc for Mortgage Loan Application

CUSTOMER

Customer ID

LOAN COLLATERAL

Loan Collateral ID
Collateral Type Code (FK) Collateral Item Text Collateral Purpose Text Collateral Value Mortgage Loan ID (FK) Customer ID (FK)

CUSTOMER/ MORTGAGE/ LOAN

Mortgage Loan ID (FK) Customer ID (FK)
Property Address Code (FK) Property Appraisal Date Appraised Property Value Mortgage Loan Amount Mortgage Loan Borrow Date Mortgage Loan End Date In Arrears Y/N Collateralized Y/N Comparable Property Address 1 Comparable Property Value 1 Comparable Property Address 2 Comparable Property Value 2 Loan Collateral ID (FK)

MORTGAGE LOAN ARREARS

Mortgage Loan Arrears ID Mortgage Loan ID (FK) Customer ID (FK)
Arrears Month Count In Arrears Initial Date Arrears Month Limit Number of Arrears Occurances

Z

Certificate of Deposit

A **Certificate of Deposit or CD** is a type of savings account offered by banks and some credit unions. A Customer generally agrees to keep their money in the CD without taking a withdrawal for a specified length of time. Withdrawing money early means paying a penalty fee to the Bank. Let's consider grafting this onto the Checking and Savings Logical ERD. The data to retain about CDs is as follows:

CD Selection Type	CD Identification
CD Amount Deposited/Face Value CD	Interest Rate
CD Term CD For the Benefit Of	CD Early Withdrawal Date
CD Start DateTime	CD Penalty for Early Withdrawal

Here is the mapping chart:

CD Attribute	Maps to, or is a Code of Entity/Attribute	New Entity, required
CD as a Banking Product	Banking Product/Banking Product Type Code (FK)	
CD Selection Type Code (FK)	Agreement/Agreement Type (FK)	
CD Selection subtype Code (FK)	Account/Account subtype (FK)	
CD Identification Number	Account/Account Number	
CD Term		Certificate of Deposit/CD Term
CD Face Value		Certificate of Deposit/CD Face Value
CD Interest Rate		Certificate of Deposit/CD Interest Rate
CD Start Date	Agreement/Agreement Start Date	
CD Early Withdrawal Date		Certificate of Deposit/CD Early Withdrawal Date
CD Interest Paid	Account/Interest Amount	
CD Total Principle plus Interest Paid		Certificate of Deposit/CD Total Principle plus Interest Paid
CD Penalty for Early Withdrawal		Certificate of Deposit/CD Penalty for Early Withdrawal
CD For the Benefit Of		Certificate of Deposit/CD For the Benefit Of
CD Interest Indicator = Y	Account/Interest Indicator = Y	
CD Interest Paid Datetime	Account/Interest Paid Datetime	

Important entities are Agreement, Account, Banking Product and Certificate of Deposit. See next ERD:

CUSTOMER/PRODUCT

Customer ID (FK)
Product ID (FK)

CUSTOMER

Customer ID

ACCOUNT

Agreement ID (FK)
Customer ID (FK)
Account Start Date
Account Type (FK)

Account Subtype (FK)
Account End Date
Account Routing Number
Account Number
Account Name
Account Payment or Deposit
Account Payment Datetime
Account Payment Day of Month
Interest Indicator Y/N
Interest Amount
Interest Paid Datetime
Overdraft Indicator Y/N
Maximum Amount of Overdraft

AGREEMENT

Agreement ID

Agreement Type (FK)
Agreement Subtype (FK)
Agreement Start Date
Agreement End Date
Agreement Risk Code (FK)
Agreement Currency Code (FK)

LINE ITEM

Line Item ID

Line Item Number
Line Item Balance
Agreement ID (FK)
Customer ID (FK)
Account Start Date (FK)
Account Type (FK) (FK)

BANKING PRODUCT

Banking Product ID (FK)

Banking Product Type Code (FK)
Banking Line of Business Code (FK)

INSURANCE PRODUCT

Insurance Product ID (FK)

Insurance Type Code (FK)

CUSTOMER/EVENT

Customer ID (FK)
Event ID (FK)

Customer Event Type (FK)
Customer Event Subtype (FK)

MORTGAGE or LOAN see above

Mortgage/Loan ID (FK)

CERTIFICATE OF DEPOSIT

CDt ID (FK)

CD Term
CD Face Value
CD Interest Rate
CD Early Withdrawal Date
CD Total Priinciple plus Interest Paid
CD Penalty for Early Withdrawal
CD For the Benefit Of

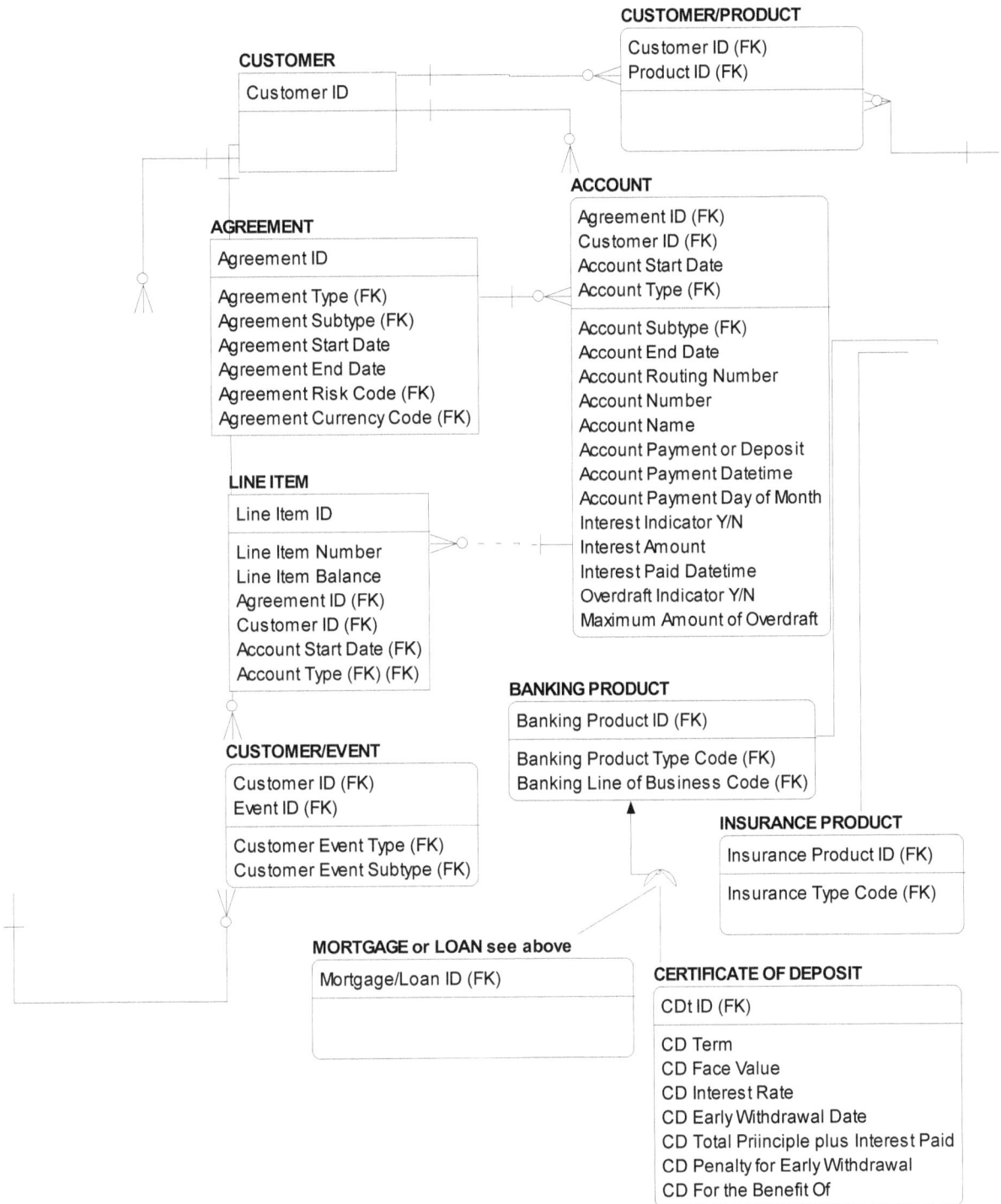

Model 10.0 Retail Banking Logical ERD partial, with Certificate of Deposit entity added.

End of Customer and Product Subject Areas in Retail Banking

Commercial Banking

A commercial bank may conduct all or some of these businesses:

Accepting deposits	Credit cash
Money (Wire) Remittance	Foreign Exchange
Commercial Lending	Exchange of Securities
Locker Facilities	Overdraft
Treasury Management	Trustee & Executor
Agent Functions	Bills of Exchange
Cash Management	Collecting Bills
Investment Management	Merchant Services
Offering Insurance	Issue Bank Drafts and Checks
Issuing Credit Cards	Trade Finance

Typically, a commercial bank will specialize in a handful of these functions. Only the largest commercial banks, such as JPMorgan Chase, Citibank, etc., have departments and staff to handle all of these functions. Therefore, when you are modeling for a Commercial Bank, find out what their objectives and areas of expertise are, else you could spend a lifetime modeling for all of this functionality.

Since there are 20 different functions that a Commercial Bank could perform, I am selecting three of the most common ones for starter attribute lists and models: Commercial Lending, Commercial Deposits, and a Banker or Banking Department acting as an Agent For.

Commercial Lending

Basic entities:

Commercial Loan Identification	
Commercial Loan Customer	Commercial Loan Customer Credit Rating
Commercial Loan Amount	Commercial Loan Start Datetime
Commercial Loan End Datetime	Commercial Loan Collateral Type
Commercial Loan Collateral Value	Commercial Loan Collateral Value Appraiser
Commercial Loan Interest Rate	Commercial Loan Customer Resp Officer 1,2

Referring back to the Retail Banking Logical ERD, and the Customer ERD, we can certainly borrow some entities

Commercial Loan requirement	Mapped to existing Retail Banking Logical entities	Create new entity/attribute
Commercial Loan Identification	Mortgage/Loan	
Commercial Loan Customer	Customer, Customer Identification, Customer Role	
Commercial Loan Customer Credit Rating	Customer Credit Rating	
Commercial Loan Amount	Customer/Mortgage/Loan	
Commercial Loan Start Date	Customer/Mortgage/Loan	
Commercial Loan End Date	Customer/Mortgage/Loan	Added attribute Mortgage Loan End Date to this entity
Commercial Loan Collateral Type	Loan Collateral	
Commercial Loan Collateral Value	Loan Collateral	
Commercial Loan Collateral Value Appraiser	Customer, Customer Role	
Commercial Loan Interest Rate	Product, Feature, Rate Feature	
Commercial Loan Customer's Responsible Officer 1	Customer. Customer Role	
Commercial Loan Customer's Responsible Officer 2	Customer, Customer Role	

Gee whiz! We only had to add one attribute to support Commercial Loans with the Retail Banking Logical ERD! Next, let's take a look at Accepting Deposits.

Accepting Commercial Deposits

The minimum set of required attributes are:

Commercial Customer Identification   Commercial Account Identification
Commercial Deposit Amount   Commercial Deposit Datetime
Commercial Deposit Bank Officer ID   USD or Other Currency

We can already see that this will be very similar to Deposits in Retail Banking.

Commercial Deposit Requirement	Mapped to existing Retail Banking Logical entities	Create new entity/attribute
Commercial Customer Identification	Customer, Customer Identification, Customer Role	
Commercial Account Identification	Account	
Commercial Deposit Amount	Account	
Commercial Deposit Datetime	Account	
Commercial Deposit Bank Officer ID	Customer. Customer Role, Customer Identification	
USD or Other Currency	Country/Currency (reference entity)	

Well, no changes at all to our Retail Banking model. Hooray! It can be used for Commercial Banking. Just make sure that you are very specific with CUSTOMER ROLE. In the list of valid values for an attribute, it is perfectly ok to list one hundred different roles, each with a distinct code.

Next, let's model Agent For.

Agent For

A Person or Firm acting as an Agent for another one.

A Person or a Firm may be empowered, with the proper legal documentation, to act as an Agent for a Bank, Group of Banks, Another Person, or a particular Business. The basic set of entities include:

Agent Identification & Role   Agent's Customer Legal Name & IDs
Agent For Start Datetime   Agent For End Date
Purpose of Agency   Agent For Legal Appointment Document
Special Instruction 1   Special Instruction 2

Let's see how it maps to our Retail Banking Logical ERD

Agent For Requirement	Mapped to Existing Retail Banking Entities	Create New Entity/Attribute
Agent Identification & Role	Customer, Customer Identification, Customer Role	Note: In CUSTOMER ROLE, spell out exactly who the Agent is working for. For example, Code 37 = Agent for Energy Division of JPMorgan Chase Inc.
Agent for Start Date		Created new attribute: Customer Role Start Date in entity Customer Role
Agent for End Date		Created new attribute: Customer Role End Date in entity Customer Role

Agent For Requirement	Mapped to Existing Retail Banking Entities	Create New Entity/Attribute
Purpose of Agency	Customer/Customer Description	
Agent for legal appointment document		Created new attribute Role Legal Appointment Document in entity Customer Role
Special Instruction		Created new entity Special Instruction

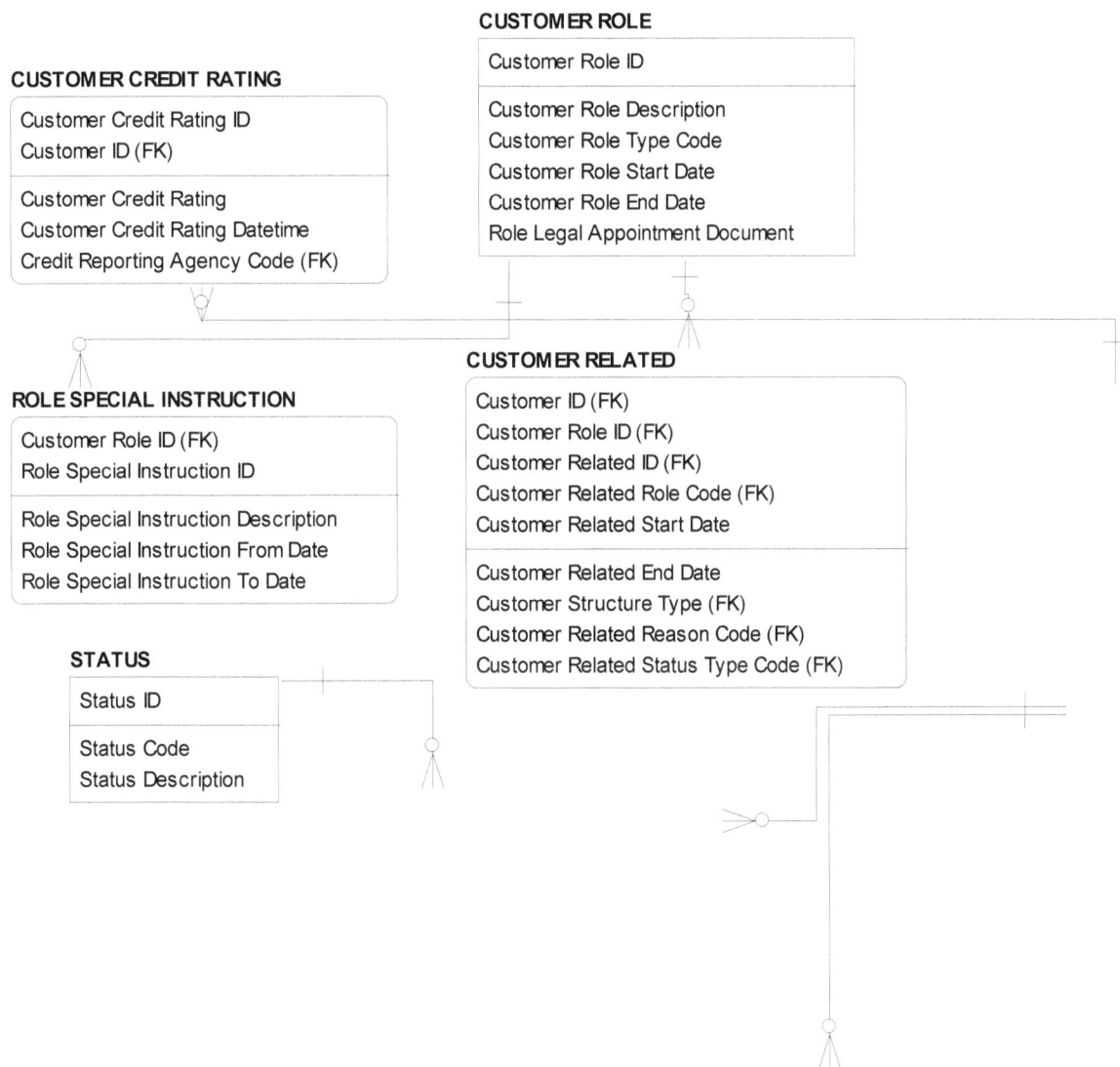

CUSTOMER ROLE

Customer Role ID

Customer Role Description
Customer Role Type Code
Customer Role Start Date
Customer Role End Date
Role Legal Appointment Document

CUSTOMER CREDIT RATING

Customer Credit Rating ID
Customer ID (FK)

Customer Credit Rating
Customer Credit Rating Datetime
Credit Reporting Agency Code (FK)

ROLE SPECIAL INSTRUCTION

Customer Role ID (FK)
Role Special Instruction ID

Role Special Instruction Description
Role Special Instruction From Date
Role Special Instruction To Date

CUSTOMER RELATED

Customer ID (FK)
Customer Role ID (FK)
Customer Related ID (FK)
Customer Related Role Code (FK)
Customer Related Start Date

Customer Related End Date
Customer Structure Type (FK)
Customer Related Reason Code (FK)
Customer Related Status Type Code (FK)

STATUS

Status ID

Status Code
Status Description

Model 11.0 'Agent For' entities and attributes added to the Customer subject area

In this fragment of the Customer Logical ERD, note the additional attributes in the entity Customer Role and the creation of the entity Role Special Instructions.

Credit Cards

A credit card for an Individual or a Firm results from an Agreement signed with a Bank or a financial institution. A Credit Card is also a Product offered by a Bank. The modeling lineage of a Credit Card Agreement from its great-great grandparent entity Agreement is as follows:

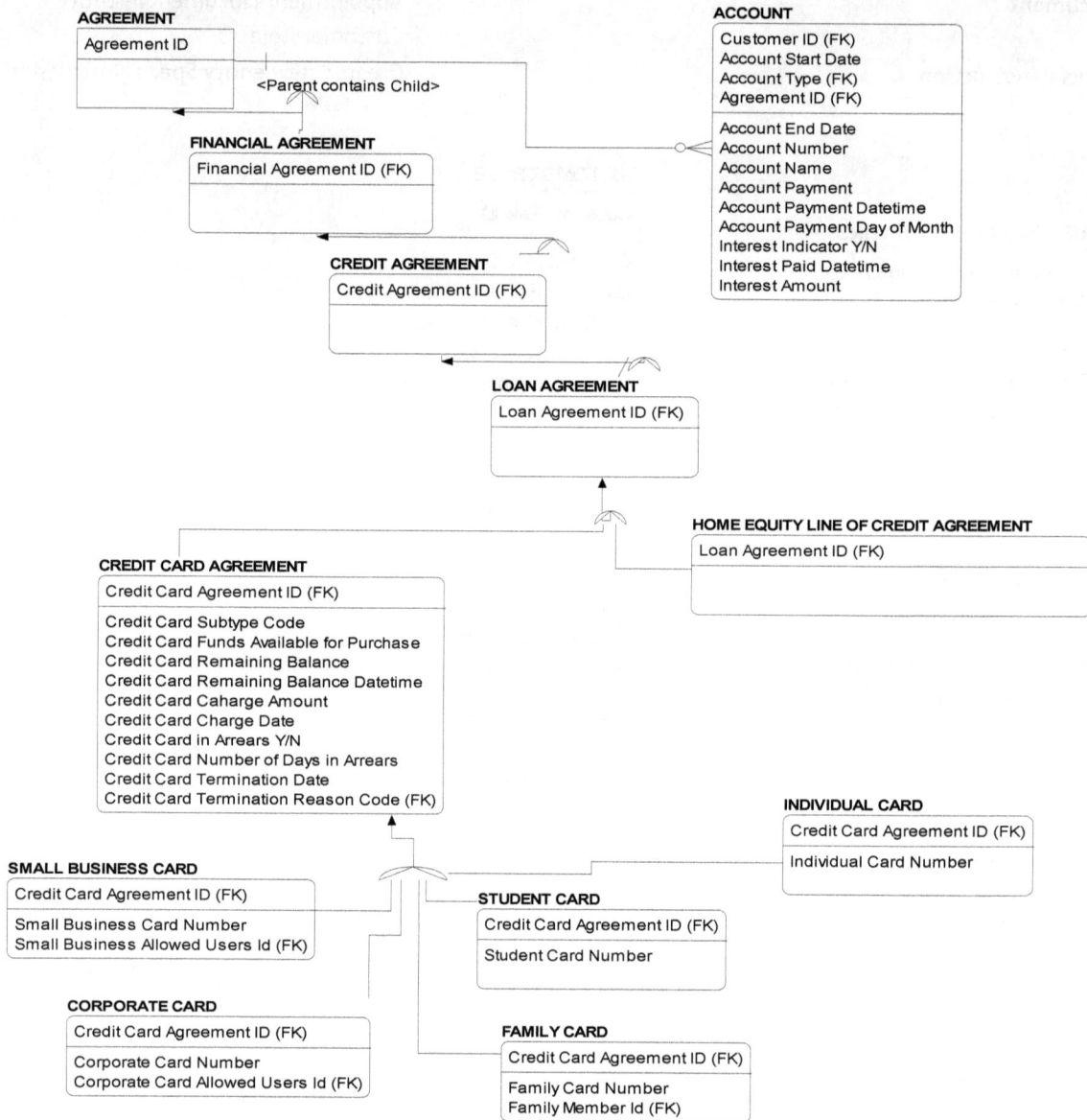

Model 12.0 Credit Card data modeling lineage from entity Agreement–

And Credit Card data model lineage from its grandparent entity Product is different:

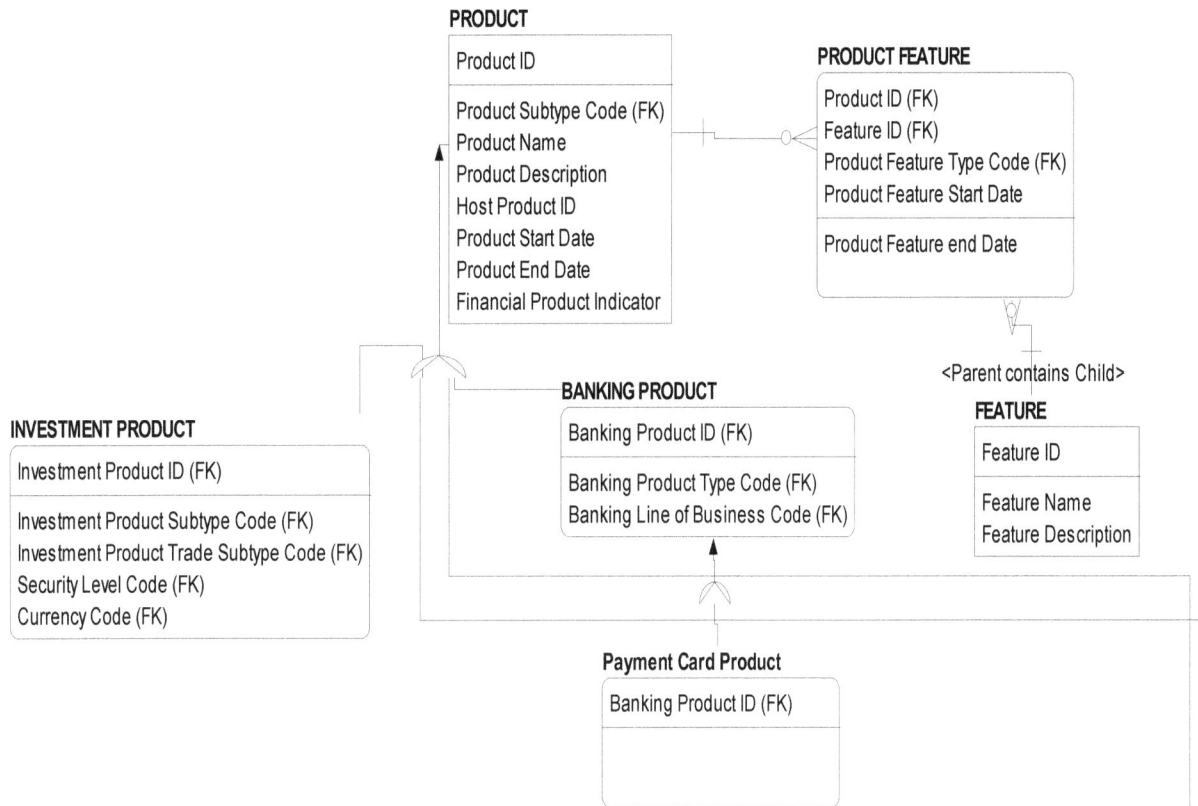

Model 13.0 Credit Card Lineage from entity Product

Now, are these business attributes associated more with the Credit Card Agreement (and Account) or the Credit Card Product?

Minimum set of Credit Card attributes:

Credit Card Type	Credit Card Number
Credit Card Upper Limit	Credit Card Interest Rate
Credit Card Funds Available for Purchase	
Credit Card Payment Day of Month	Credit Card Payment Date
Credit Card Payment	Credit Card Remaining Balance
Credit Card Charge Amount	Credit Card in Arrears (Y/N)
Credit Card Number of Days in Arrears	Credit Card Charge Date
Credit Card Special Offer	Credit Card Product Start/End Dates
Credit Card Product Name	Credit Card Annual Fee
Credit Card Terms	Credit Card Customer Start/End Dates
Credit Card Termination Date	Credit Card Termination Reason Code

Here is my take on the question. Your opinion may differ!

Attribute	Does this attribute originate from the Agreement with the Customer or from the Product designed by the Bank?
Credit Card Type	Product
Credit Card Number	Agreement & Account
Credit Card Upper Limit	Product
Credit Card Interest Rate	Product
Credit Card Funds Available for Purchases	Agreement & Account
Credit Card Payment Day of Month	Agreement & Account
Credit Card Payment	Agreement & Account
Credit Card Payment Date	Agreement & Account
Credit Card Remaining Balance	Agreement & Account
Credit Card Charge Amount	Agreement & Account
Credit Card Charge Date	Agreement & Account
Credit Card in Arrears (Y/N)	Agreement & Account
Credit Card Number of Days in Arrears	Agreement & Account
Credit Card Special Offer	Product
Credit Card Product Start/End Dates	Product
Credit Card Customer Start/End Dates	Agreement & Account
Credit Card Product Name	Product
Credit Card Annual Fee	Product
Credit Card Terms	Product
Credit Card Termination Date	Agreement & Account
Credit Card Termination Reason Code	Agreement & Account

So now let's populate the models. First, Agreement—many of these attributes are included in the entity Account. The Credit Card attributes that are not included in Account can either be added to the entity Account or can be added to the entity Credit Card Agreement. Here, I chose to add them to the entity Credit Card Agreement to keep both entities readable. Also, the attributes assigned to the entity Credit Card Agreement are dependent on the key of the entity. In contrast, the attributes in the entity Account are more generic and are used for several Banking/Credit/Loan applications.

Here is the new and improved **Model 14.0** Agreement Logical ERD for Credit Cards:

AGREEMENT
Agreement ID

<Parent contains Child>

FINANCIAL AGREEMENT
Financial Agreement ID (FK)

CREDIT AGREEMENT
Credit Agreement ID (FK)

ACCOUNT
Customer ID (FK)
Account Start Date
Account Type (FK)
Agreement ID (FK)

Account End Date
Account Number
Account Name
Account Payment
Account Payment Datetime
Account Payment Day of Month
Interest Indicator Y/N
Interest Paid Datetime
Interest Amount

CREDIT CARD AGREEMENT
Credit Card Agreement ID (FK)

Credit Card Subtype Code
Credit Card Funds Available for Purchase
Credit Card Remaining Balance
Credit Card Remaining Balance Datetime
Credit Card Caharge Amount
Credit Card Charge Date
Credit Card in Arrears Y/N
Credit Card Number of Days in Arrears
Credit Card Termination Date
Credit Card Termination Reason Code (FK)

LOAN AGREEMENT
Loan Agreement ID (FK)

HOME EQUITY LINE OF CREDIT AGREEMENT
Loan Agreement ID (FK)

INDIVIDUAL CARD
Credit Card Agreement ID (FK)

Individual Card Number

SMALL BUSINESS CARD
Credit Card Agreement ID (FK)

Small Business Card Number
Small Business Allowed Users Id (FK)

CORPORATE CARD
Credit Card Agreement ID (FK)

Corporate Card Number
Corporate Card Allowed Users Id (FK)

STUDENT CARD
Credit Card Agreement ID (FK)

Student Card Number

FAMILY CARD
Credit Card Agreement ID (FK)

Family Card Number
Family Member Id (FK)

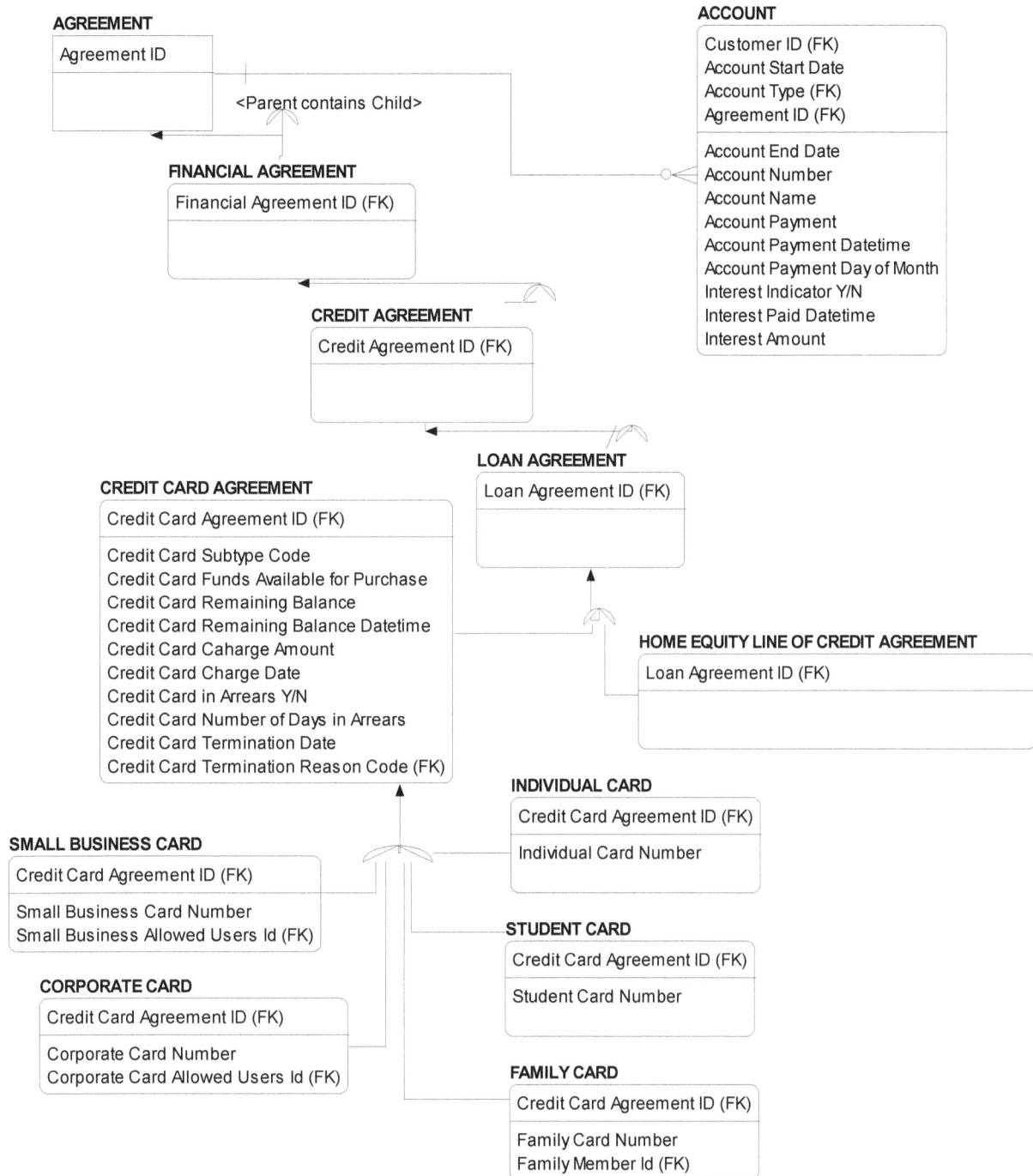

Model 14.0 Agreement Logical ERD for Credit Cards:

Now for the Product modeling for Credit Cards. The entity Payment Card Product is specifically about the Product. In this case, a credit card offering created by a Bank or a Financial Firm. There is no Customer-generated event here. This entity Payment Card Product strictly describes the Product as offered by the bank. You may need to add your unique attributes here.

In addition, some of the suggested attributes, such as Credit Card Start and End Dates, Credit Card Terms, etc., can be found in the entity Feature subtypes. Take a look at the Feature subtypes to see where to map the Credit Card attributes.

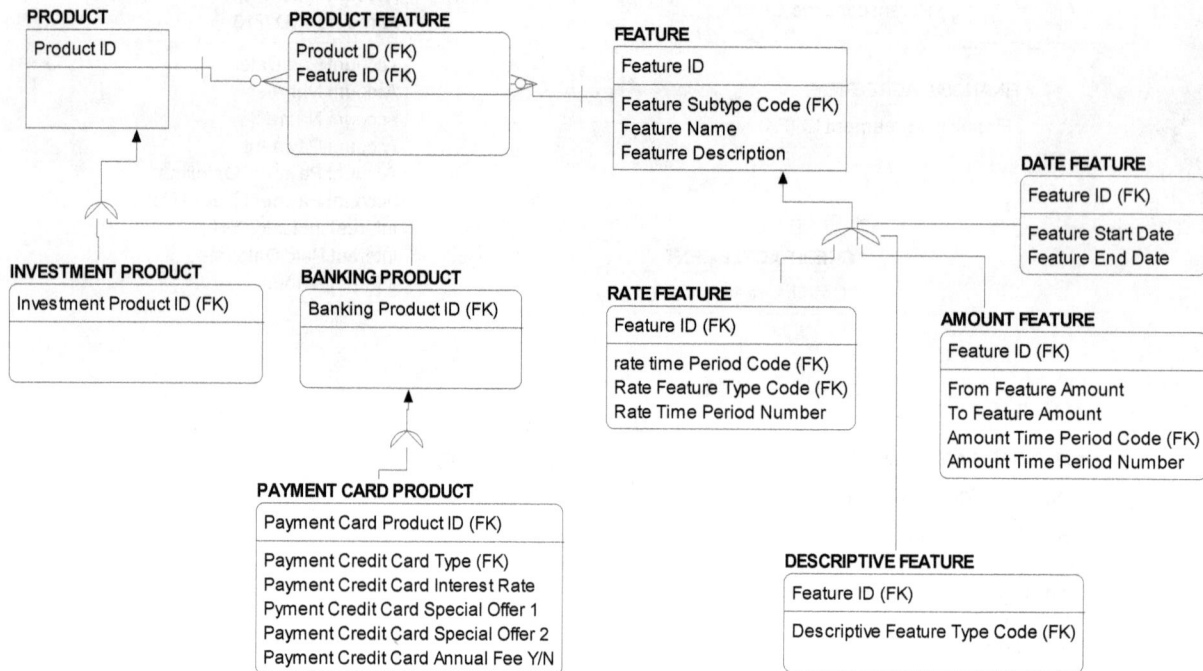

Model 15.0 Product side of the Logical ERD for Credit Cards

FIVE

Stock Brokerage/Trade Processing/Investments

This section will be called Investment for short. Wall Street firms are referred to as stock brokerage, trade processing firms, or investment houses. However you refer to them, their job is to make a profit by buying and selling stocks and bonds. Their customers are defined as our definition of Customer, plus those who have opened at least one trading account with the investment firm.

We store each Buy or Sell in the Firm's database(s). How are the transactions identified? Beginning in 1792, you could only buy stock at the New York Stock Exchange (NYSE). The first sovereign Treasury Bonds were sold to finance our Revolutionary War, but they were sold by Hayim Solomon from a table at a coffeehouse in Philadelphia. Government and corporate bond sales were migrated to exchanges after World War I.

Now, think about it: if you could design a database for stocks and bonds in 1917, your entity Investment Product would need only one attribute: Equity Y/N. If the answer were Y, you would send it down the (coded) path for stock processing, storage, and reporting. If the answer was N, you would transmit it down a path for bonds.

Investment Products or instruments are a lot more complicated now. The Waterfall Product model (below on the left) was the only necessary part of a brokerage product data model, even until recent decades. The reason is that market instruments used to fall into neat, separate categories of Equities, Fixed Income, and Options. This is no longer the case.

The largest brokerage firms have developed hybrid instruments to provide alternatives to traditional investments without sacrificing some of their benefits. When an instrument comes in the door of a trading firm, whether it is a buy, a sell, or a quotation, after it passes security checks, the first job of the database is to determine what it is.

Therefore, **the FEATURES subject area (below on the right) is utilized first along with entity Product Identification to ascertain which instrument the customer is buying or selling,** and then it is stored in the Waterfall....in the appropriate bucket.

High level entities in the Waterfall (type of Investment) include:

Equity	Bond	Option
Commodity	Derivative	Mutual Fund
Exchange Traded Fund	Cash Equivalent	Money Market Fund
Certificate of Deposit	Index Fund	REIT
Alternative Investment	Currency Contract	

Note that Currency Contracts must also be modeled under entity Agreement which has a subtype of entity Investment Agreement that is subtyped to entity Foreign Exchange Agreement. (Not modeled here).

A very high-level view of the Investments scenario is as follows:

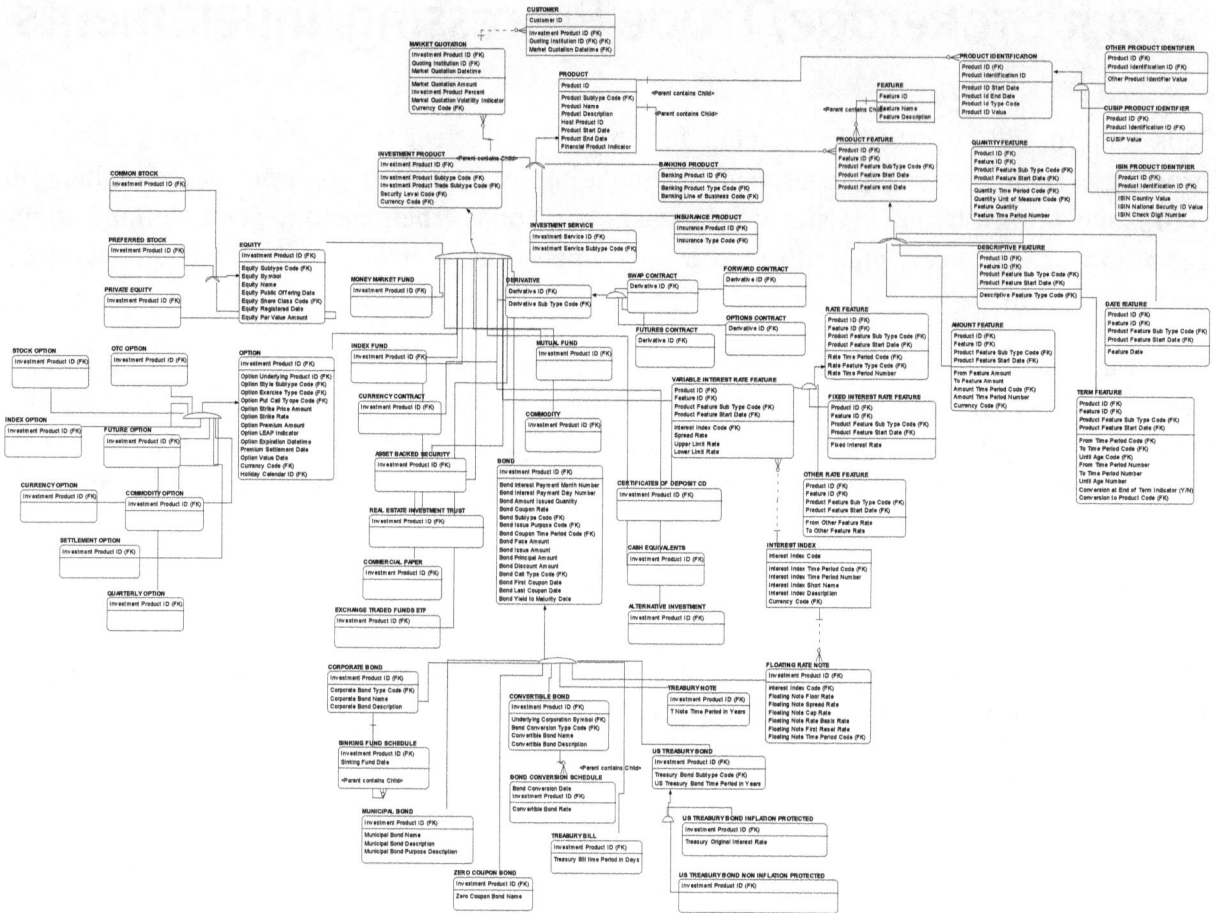

Model 16.0 High Level View of Investment Logical ERD

Well, again this is difficult to read, so we will look at it in two sections. First, the primary entities on the left side, which is the Waterfall and then the right side, which is the Features section.

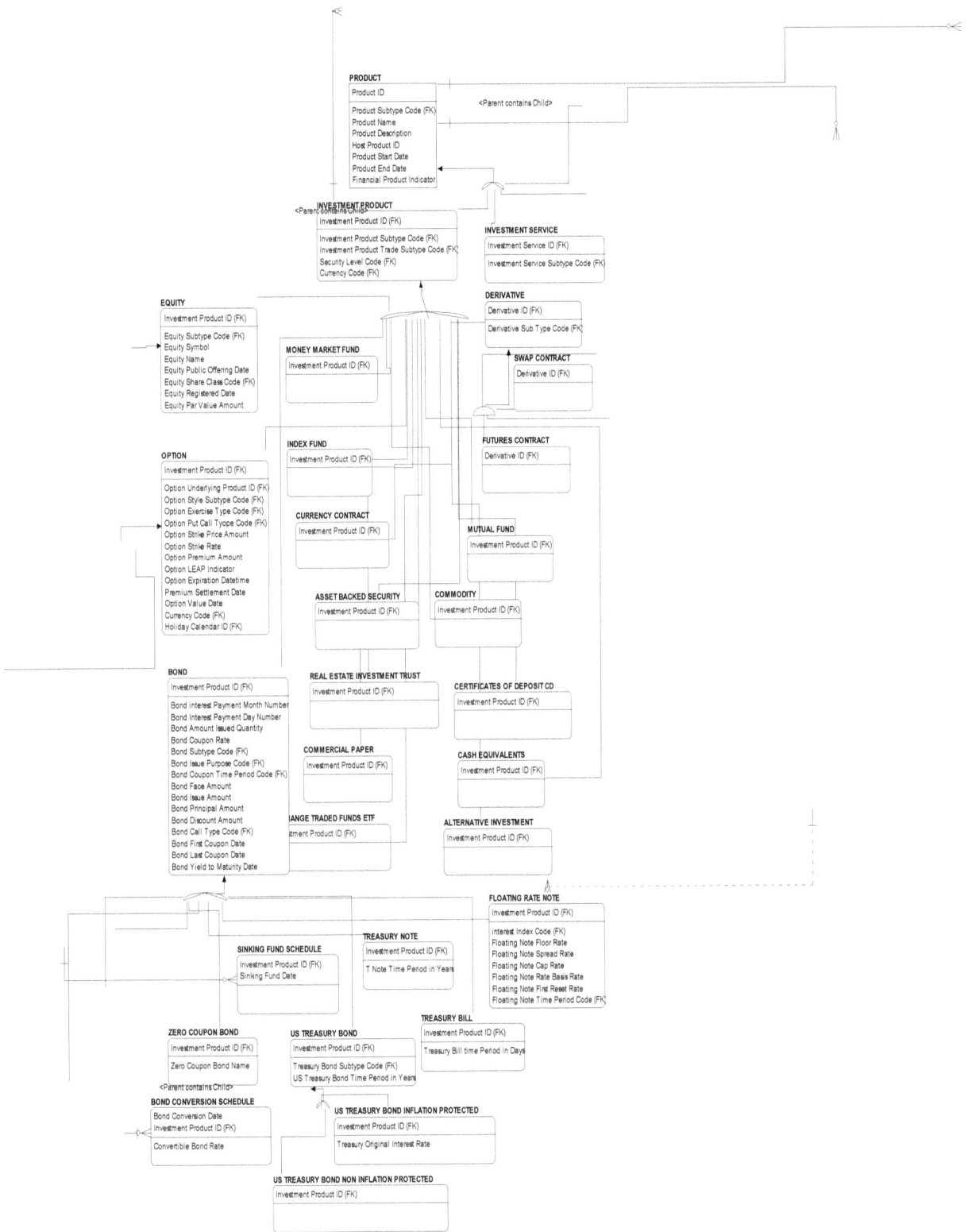

PRODUCT
Product ID

Product Subtype Code (FK)
Product Name
Product Description
Host Product ID
Product Start Date
Product End Date
Financial Product Indicator

<Parent contains Child>

INVESTMENT PRODUCT
Investment Product ID (FK)

Investment Product Subtype Code (FK)
Investment Product Trade Subtype Code (FK)
Security Level Code (FK)
Currency Code (FK)

INVESTMENT SERVICE
Investment Service ID (FK)

Investment Service Subtype Code (FK)

EQUITY
Investment Product ID (FK)

Equity Subtype Code (FK)
Equity Symbol
Equity Name
Equity Public Offering Date
Equity Share Class Code (FK)
Equity Registered Date
Equity Par Value Amount

MONEY MARKET FUND
Investment Product ID (FK)

DERIVATIVE
Derivative ID (FK)

Derivative Sub Type Code (FK)

SWAP CONTRACT
Derivative ID (FK)

OPTION
Investment Product ID (FK)

Option Underlying Product ID (FK)
Option Style Subtype Code (FK)
Option Exercise Type Code (FK)
Option Put Call Type Code (FK)
Option Strike Price Amount
Option Strike Rate
Option Premium Amount
Option LEAP Indicator
Option Expiration Datetime
Premium Settlement Date
Option Value Date
Currency Code (FK)
Holiday Calendar ID (FK)

INDEX FUND
Investment Product ID (FK)

FUTURES CONTRACT
Derivative ID (FK)

CURRENCY CONTRACT
Investment Product ID (FK)

MUTUAL FUND
Investment Product ID (FK)

ASSET BACKED SECURITY
Investment Product ID (FK)

COMMODITY
Investment Product ID (FK)

BOND
Investment Product ID (FK)

Bond Interest Payment Month Number
Bond Interest Payment Day Number
Bond Amount Issued Quantity
Bond Coupon Rate
Bond Subtype Code (FK)
Bond Issue Purpose Code (FK)
Bond Coupon Time Period Code (FK)
Bond Face Amount
Bond Issue Amount
Bond Principal Amount
Bond Discount Amount
Bond Call Type Code (FK)
Bond First Coupon Date
Bond Last Coupon Date
Bond Yield to Maturity Date

REAL ESTATE INVESTMENT TRUST
Investment Product ID (FK)

CERTIFICATES OF DEPOSIT CD
Investment Product ID (FK)

COMMERCIAL PAPER
Investment Product ID (FK)

CASH EQUIVALENTS
Investment Product ID (FK)

EXCHANGE TRADED FUNDS ETF
Investment Product ID (FK)

ALTERNATIVE INVESTMENT
Investment Product ID (FK)

FLOATING RATE NOTE
Investment Product ID (FK)

Interest Index Code (FK)
Floating Note Floor Rate
Floating Note Spread Rate
Floating Note Cap Rate
Floating Note Rate Basis Rate
Floating Note First Reset Rate
Floating Note Time Period Code (FK)

SINKING FUND SCHEDULE
Investment Product ID (FK)
Sinking Fund Date

TREASURY NOTE
Investment Product ID (FK)

T Note Time Period in Years

TREASURY BILL
Investment Product ID (FK)

Treasury Bill time Period in Days

ZERO COUPON BOND
Investment Product ID (FK)

Zero Coupon Bond Name

<Parent contains Child>

US TREASURY BOND
Investment Product ID (FK)

Treasury Bond Subtype Code (FK)
US Treasury Bond Time Period in Years

BOND CONVERSION SCHEDULE
Bond Conversion Date
Investment Product ID (FK)

Convertible Bond Rate

US TREASURY BOND INFLATION PROTECTED
Investment Product ID (FK)

Treasury Original Interest Rate

US TREASURY BOND NON INFLATION PROTECTED
Investment Product ID (FK)

Model 16.01 Left side, showing the Investment Product Waterfall

Better.

Still on the left side, for further detail of Equities, Options, and Bonds:

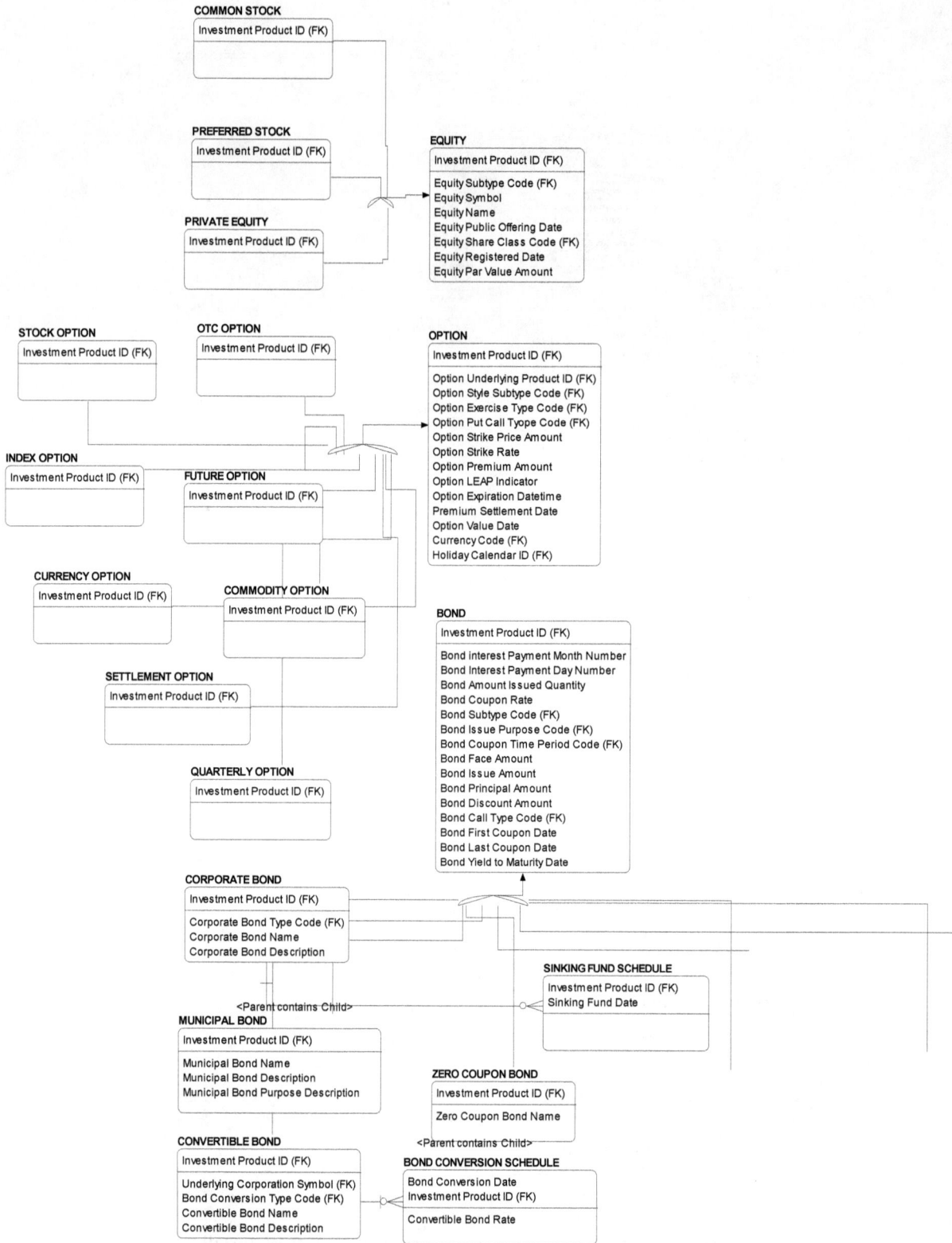

COMMON STOCK
Investment Product ID (FK)

PREFERRED STOCK
Investment Product ID (FK)

PRIVATE EQUITY
Investment Product ID (FK)

EQUITY
Investment Product ID (FK)

Equity Subtype Code (FK)
Equity Symbol
Equity Name
Equity Public Offering Date
Equity Share Class Code (FK)
Equity Registered Date
Equity Par Value Amount

STOCK OPTION
Investment Product ID (FK)

OTC OPTION
Investment Product ID (FK)

OPTION
Investment Product ID (FK)

Option Underlying Product ID (FK)
Option Style Subtype Code (FK)
Option Exercise Type Code (FK)
Option Put Call Tyope Code (FK)
Option Strike Price Amount
Option Strike Rate
Option Premium Amount
Option LEAP Indicator
Option Expiration Datetime
Premium Settlement Date
Option Value Date
Currency Code (FK)
Holiday Calendar ID (FK)

INDEX OPTION
Investment Product ID (FK)

FUTURE OPTION
Investment Product ID (FK)

CURRENCY OPTION
Investment Product ID (FK)

COMMODITY OPTION
Investment Product ID (FK)

BOND
Investment Product ID (FK)

Bond interest Payment Month Number
Bond Interest Payment Day Number
Bond Amount Issued Quantity
Bond Coupon Rate
Bond Subtype Code (FK)
Bond Issue Purpose Code (FK)
Bond Coupon Time Period Code (FK)
Bond Face Amount
Bond Issue Amount
Bond Principal Amount
Bond Discount Amount
Bond Call Type Code (FK)
Bond First Coupon Date
Bond Last Coupon Date
Bond Yield to Maturity Date

SETTLEMENT OPTION
Investment Product ID (FK)

QUARTERLY OPTION
Investment Product ID (FK)

CORPORATE BOND
Investment Product ID (FK)

Corporate Bond Type Code (FK)
Corporate Bond Name
Corporate Bond Description

<Parent contains Child>

SINKING FUND SCHEDULE
Investment Product ID (FK)
Sinking Fund Date

MUNICIPAL BOND
Investment Product ID (FK)

Municipal Bond Name
Municipal Bond Description
Municipal Bond Purpose Description

ZERO COUPON BOND
Investment Product ID (FK)

Zero Coupon Bond Name

<Parent contains Child>

CONVERTIBLE BOND
Investment Product ID (FK)

Underlying Corporation Symbol (FK)
Bond Conversion Type Code (FK)
Convertible Bond Name
Convertible Bond Description

BOND CONVERSION SCHEDULE
Bond Conversion Date
Investment Product ID (FK)

Convertible Bond Rate

Model 16.01a Equities, Options and Bonds

Next, we'll look at the right side of model 16.0, model 16.02, Product Feature, which determines what the Product is. In other words, the Product's features determine which type of Product it is.

Model 16.02 Feature side of Investment Product

The right side of **Model 16.0** is a high-level view of entity Product and its relationship to entity Features. As the investment world develops instruments with new or additional features, tests for those features can be added as entities here.

Next, we'll look at a really detailed Logical model for Investments. This model is not complete, by any means. Only about one-half of the Option types appear. Three Investment products are also not modeled here: Medium Term Notes, Securities Index Products, and Financial Instrument Groups.

Where you see unpopulated entities, it is your opportunity to attribute the entity with the facts that are important to your business. Now, here is the really detailed Logical ERD for Stock Brokerage/Trade Processing/Investments:

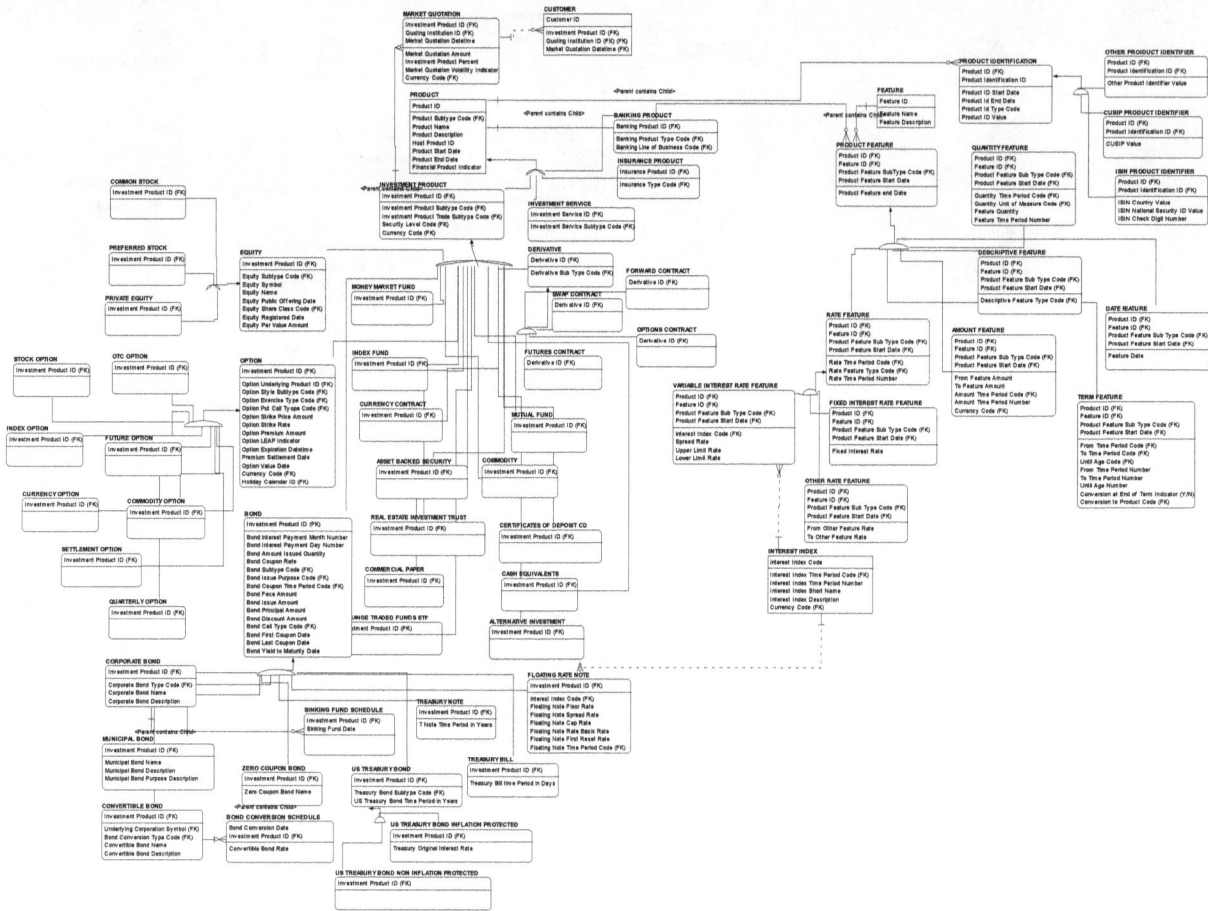

Model 16.03 *Very Detailed* Investment Logical ERD

Well, this is the whole starter mode all right, but no one can read it. Let's start with the left side first: Equity and Option: The next page has **Model 16.03a Equity and Option:**

COMMON STOCK

Investment Product ID (FK)

PREFERRED STOCK

Investment Product ID (FK)

EQUITY

Investment Product ID (FK)

Equity Subtype Code (FK)
Equity Symbol
Equity Name
Equity Public Offering Date
Equity Share Class Code (FK)
Equity Registered Date
Equity Par Value Amount

PRIVATE EQUITY

Investment Product ID (FK)

STOCK OPTION

Investment Product ID (FK)

OTC OPTION

Investment Product ID (FK)

OPTION

Investment Product ID (FK)

Option Underlying Product ID (FK)
Option Style Subtype Code (FK)
Option Exercise Type Code (FK)
Option Put Call Tyope Code (FK)
Option Strike Price Amount
Option Strike Rate
Option Premium Amount
Option LEAP Indicator
Option Expiration Datetime
Premium Settlement Date
Option Value Date
Holiday Calendar ID (FK)

INDEX OPTION

Investment Product ID (FK)

FUTURE OPTION

Investment Product ID (FK)

CURRENCY OPTION

Investment Product ID (FK)

COMMODITY OPTION

Investment Product ID (FK)

SETTLEMENT OPTION

Investment Product ID (FK)

QUARTERLY OPTION

Investment Product ID (FK)

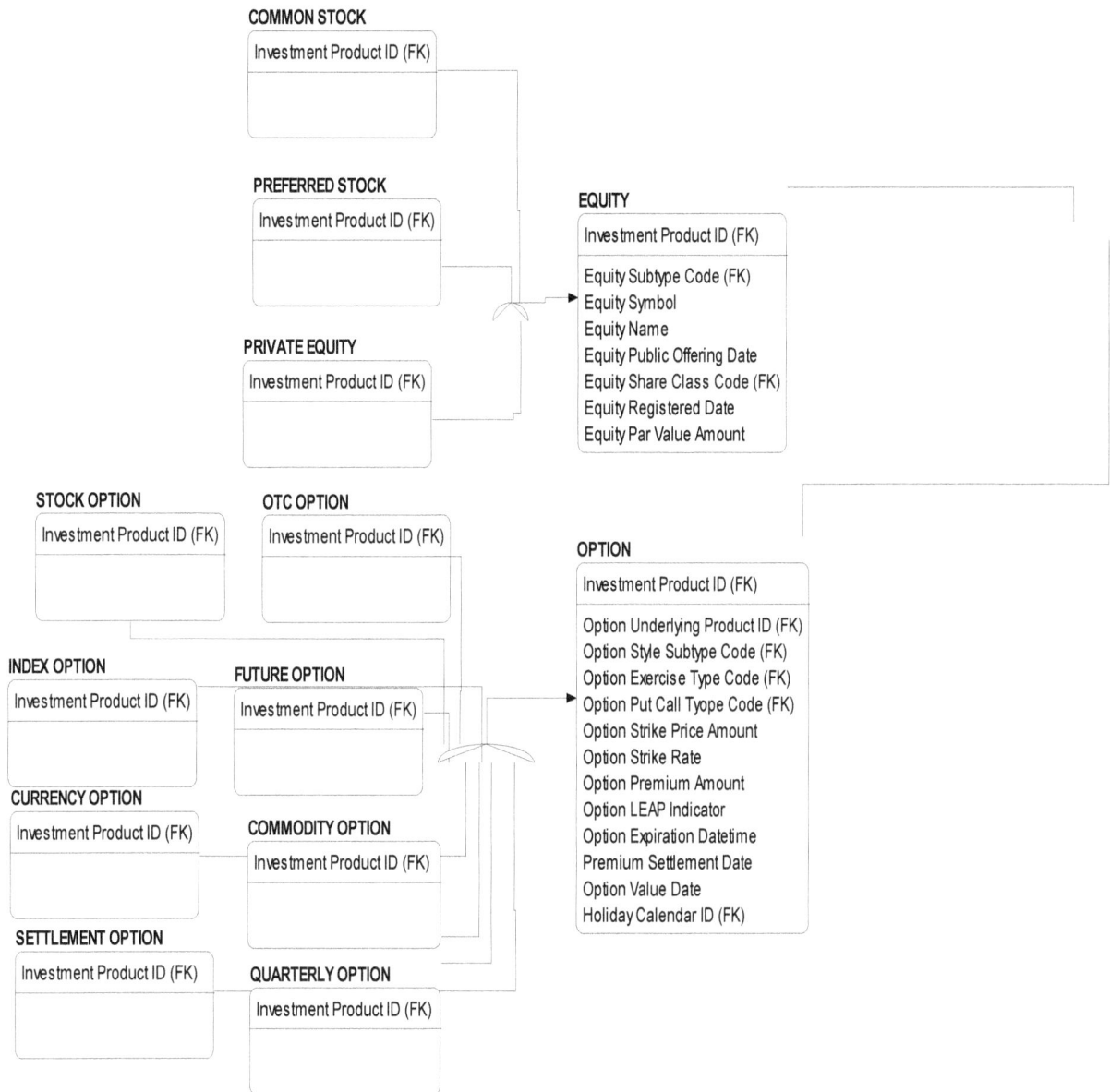

Model 16.03a Equities and Options

On the next page are the details of a starter model for Bonds:

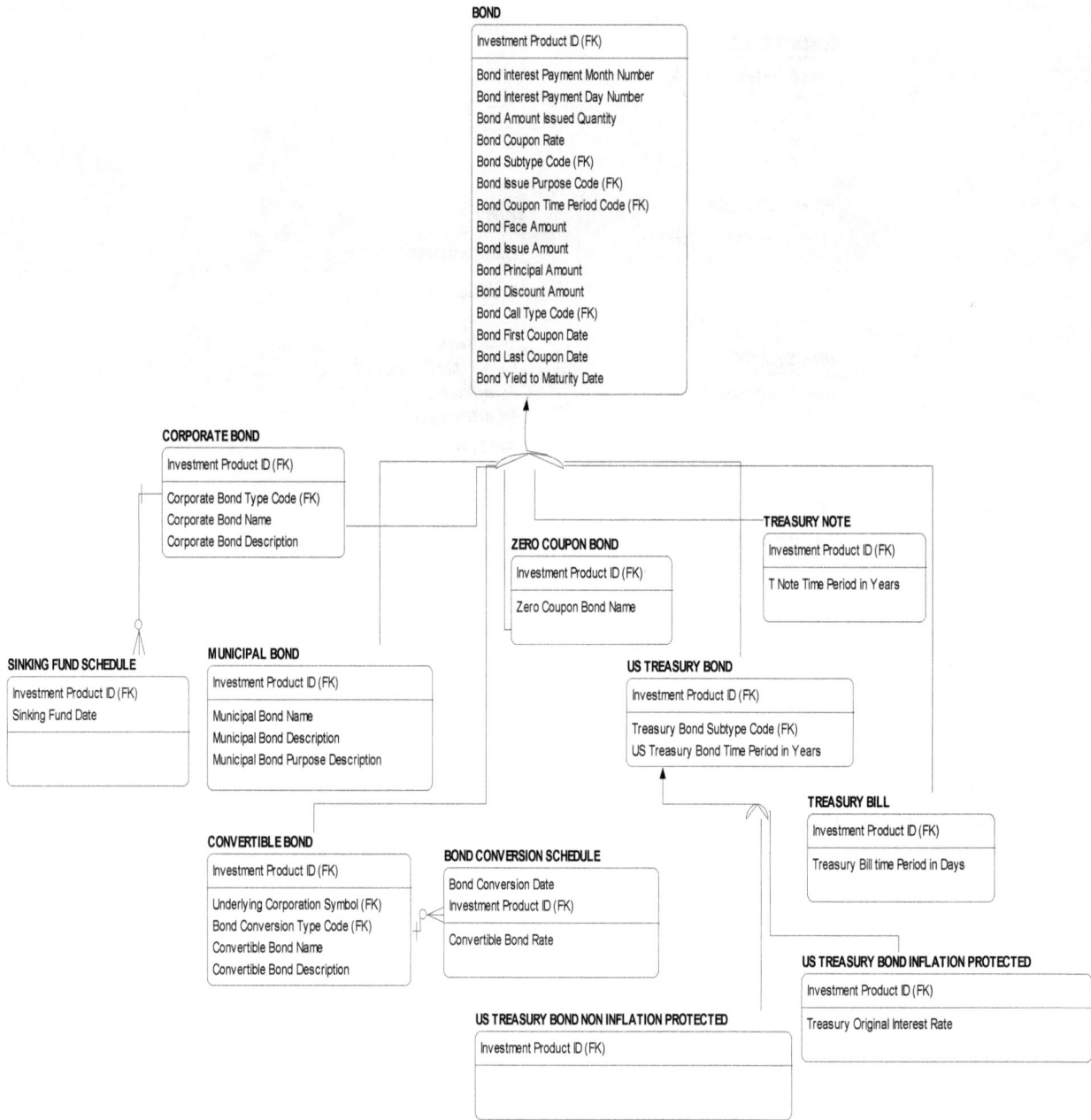

Model 16.03b Bonds

Next, let's look at the top middle of the model, where we can see the entity Investment Product.

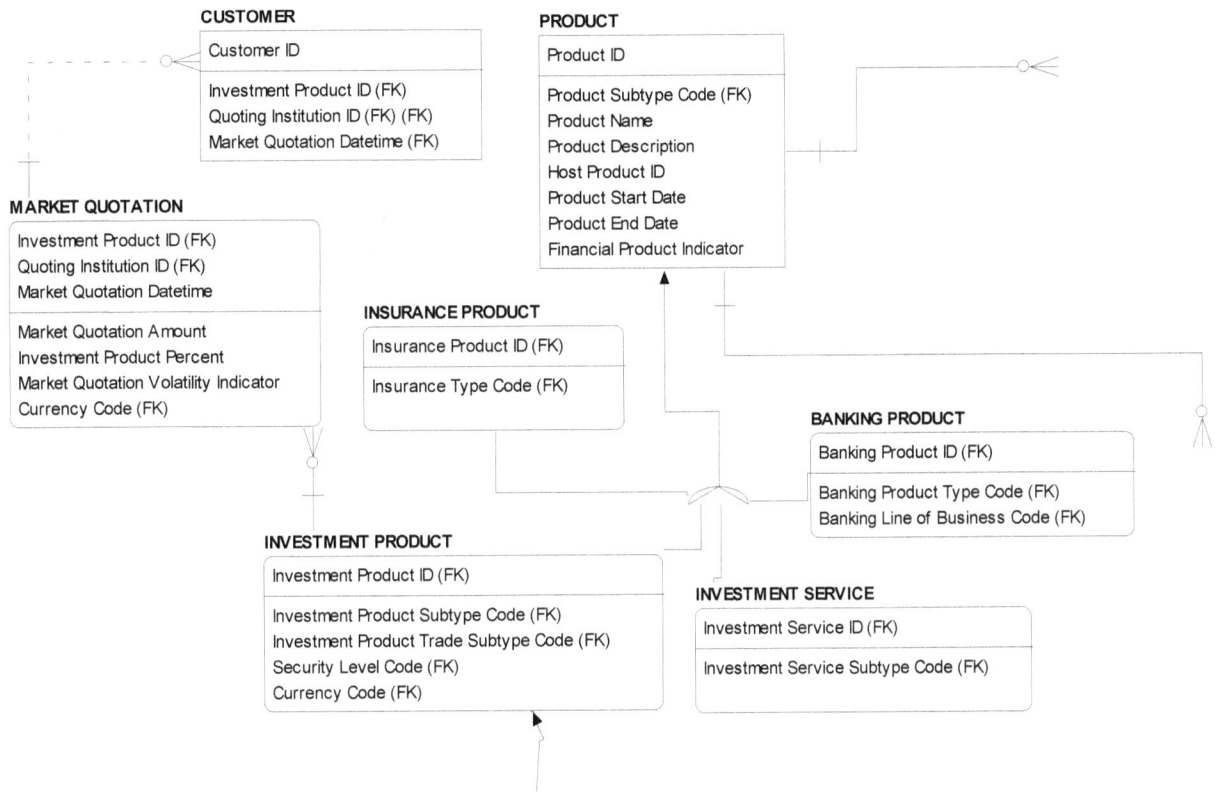

Model 16.04 Investment Product section of the Investment Logical ERD

These entities are the management structure that enable this logical model to categorize instrument features and type of Product. The upper relationship from Product goes to Product Feature, and that entity has a relationship with Feature. Using the Feature entity and its subtypes (some of which you may add) we can select the features which appear on the instrument in question, thus categorizing it, and enabling the Product entity to store a full set of its characteristics.

Now, let's look at the subtypes of Entity Investment Product in **Model 16.05:**

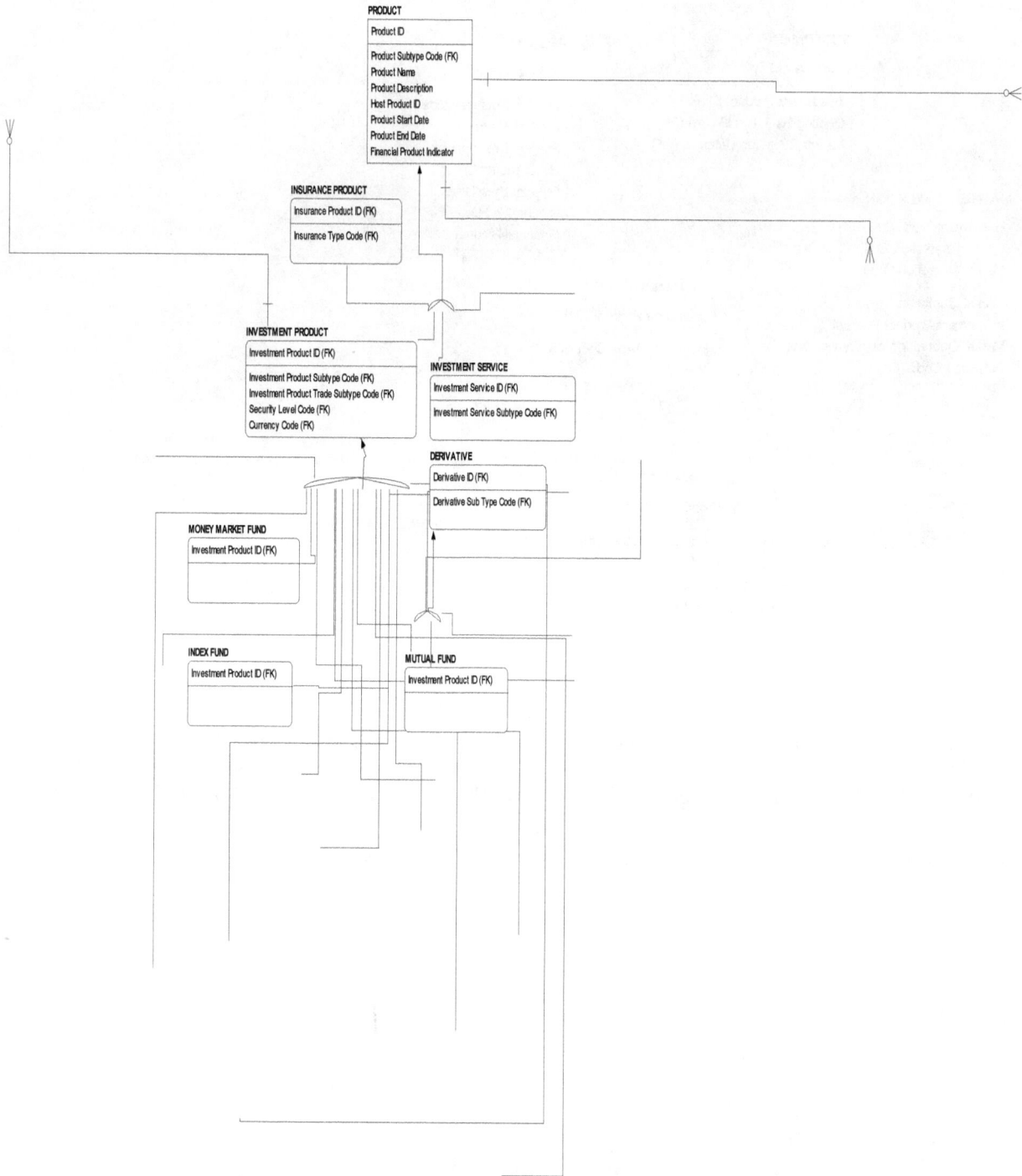

Model 16.05 Subtypes of Entity Investment Product

Above, we see four major subtypes of entity Investment Product - Derivative, Index Fund, Money Market Fund and Mutual Fund. There are many more subtypes. Not including Equities Options and Bonds, there are 13 more subtypes of Investment Product that appear in the model below.

Note that as the NYSE and the Nasdaq continue working with the top brokerage firms, new subtypes may be added. Different and unique investment vehicles are available on Japanese markets, but they will not be discussed here.

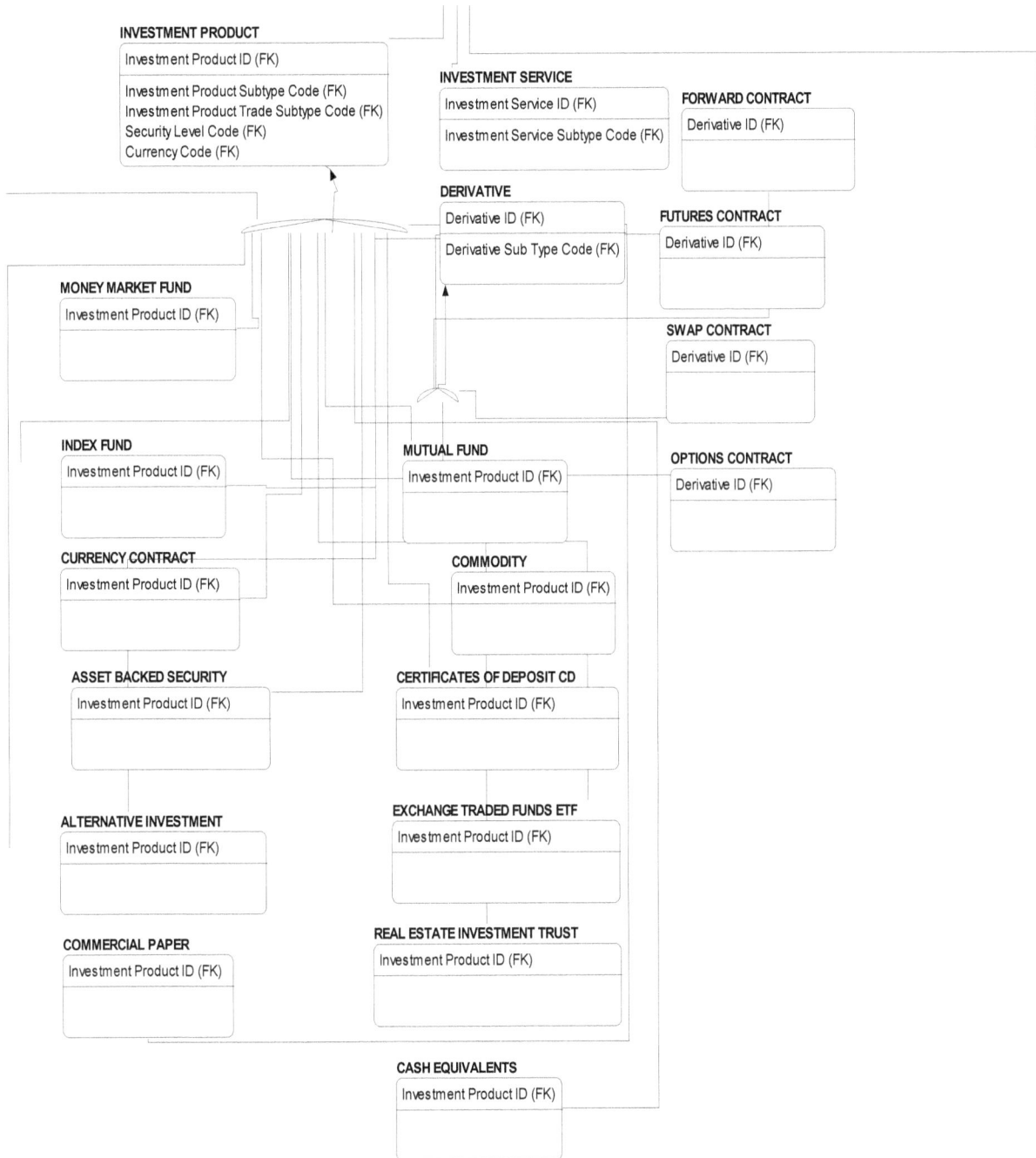

INVESTMENT PRODUCT
- Investment Product ID (FK)
- Investment Product Subtype Code (FK)
- Investment Product Trade Subtype Code (FK)
- Security Level Code (FK)
- Currency Code (FK)

INVESTMENT SERVICE
- Investment Service ID (FK)
- Investment Service Subtype Code (FK)

FORWARD CONTRACT
- Derivative ID (FK)

DERIVATIVE
- Derivative ID (FK)
- Derivative Sub Type Code (FK)

FUTURES CONTRACT
- Derivative ID (FK)

MONEY MARKET FUND
- Investment Product ID (FK)

SWAP CONTRACT
- Derivative ID (FK)

INDEX FUND
- Investment Product ID (FK)

MUTUAL FUND
- Investment Product ID (FK)

OPTIONS CONTRACT
- Derivative ID (FK)

CURRENCY CONTRACT
- Investment Product ID (FK)

COMMODITY
- Investment Product ID (FK)

ASSET BACKED SECURITY
- Investment Product ID (FK)

CERTIFICATES OF DEPOSIT CD
- Investment Product ID (FK)

ALTERNATIVE INVESTMENT
- Investment Product ID (FK)

EXCHANGE TRADED FUNDS ETF
- Investment Product ID (FK)

COMMERCIAL PAPER
- Investment Product ID (FK)

REAL ESTATE INVESTMENT TRUST
- Investment Product ID (FK)

CASH EQUIVALENTS
- Investment Product ID (FK)

<u>Model 16.06</u> **Thirteen subtypes of Entity Investment Product**

Next, we will move to the right of entity Investment Product and look at more entities under Product and Product Feature. See next page.

Below entity Product Feature, we see the first feature which is entity Rate Feature. Rate Feature has three subtypes: Fixed Interest Rate Feature, Variable Interest Rate Feature and Other Rate Feature. Read more about FEATURE below.

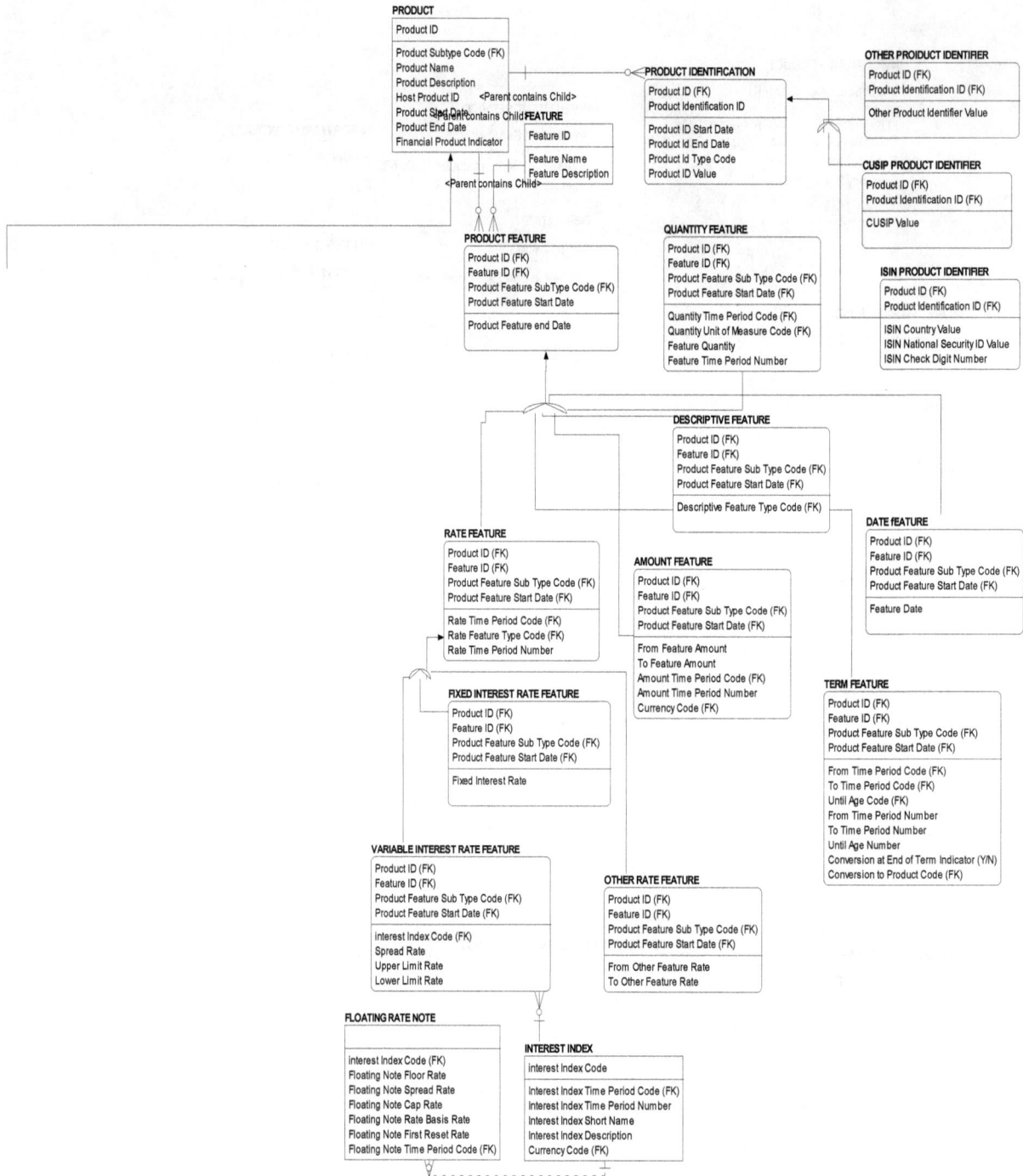

Model 16.07 Product and Product Feature of Investment Product subject area

Note that the entity Product Identification is also included in this model in the upper right-hand corner with its subtypes.

Feature – The Features or "designed characteristics" of an investment Instrument determine its classification as an Equity or a Fixed Income or an Option or Other Instrument. With the rise of custom/specialized investment instruments, it is important to examine the features of an instrument first, as it comes in the door of the Firm, determine which features it is exhibiting, and then, subsequently classify it into an entity in the Waterfall (type of instrument) schema. Entities in the Feature subject area include:

Quantity Feature	Rate Feature
Descriptive Feature	Term Feature
Date Feature	Amount Feature

You may need to add a Custom Features, depending on your Business Requirements. Below is the Entity Product Feature and its subtypes:

PRODUCT FEATURE

Product ID (FK)
Feature ID (FK)
Product Feature SubType Code (FK)
Product Feature Start Date

Product Feature end Date

QUANTITY FEATURE

Product ID (FK)
Feature ID (FK)
Product Feature Sub Type Code (FK)
Product Feature Start Date (FK)

Quantity Time Period Code (FK)
Quantity Unit of Measure Code (FK)
Feature Quantity
Feature Time Period Number

DESCRIPTIVE FEATURE

Product ID (FK)
Feature ID (FK)
Product Feature Sub Type Code (FK)
Product Feature Start Date (FK)

Descriptive Feature Type Code (FK)

RATE FEATURE

Product ID (FK)
Feature ID (FK)
Product Feature Sub Type Code (FK)
Product Feature Start Date (FK)

Rate Time Period Code (FK)
Rate Feature Type Code (FK)
Rate Time Period Number

AMOUNT FEATURE

Product ID (FK)
Feature ID (FK)
Product Feature Sub Type Code (FK)
Product Feature Start Date (FK)

From Feature Amount
To Feature Amount
Amount Time Period Code (FK)
Amount Time Period Number
Currency Code (FK)

DATE fEATURE

Product ID (FK)
Feature ID (FK)
Product Feature Sub Type Code (FK)
Product Feature Start Date (FK)

Feature Date

FIXED INTEREST RATE FEATURE

Product ID (FK)
Feature ID (FK)
Product Feature Sub Type Code (FK)
Product Feature Start Date (FK)

Fixed Interest Rate

TERM FEATURE

Product ID (FK)
Feature ID (FK)
Product Feature Sub Type Code (FK)
Product Feature Start Date (FK)

From Time Period Code (FK)
To Time Period Code (FK)
Until Age Code (FK)
From Time Period Number
To Time Period Number
Until Age Number
Conversion at End of Term Indicator (Y/N)
Conversion to Product Code (FK)

VARIABLE INTEREST RATE FEATURE

Product ID (FK)
Feature ID (FK)
Product Feature Sub Type Code (FK)
Product Feature Start Date (FK)

interest Index Code (FK)
Spread Rate
Upper Limit Rate
Lower Limit Rate

OTHER RATE FEATURE

Product ID (FK)
Feature ID (FK)
Product Feature Sub Type Code (FK)
Product Feature Start Date (FK)

From Other Feature Rate
To Other Feature Rate

FLOATING RATE NOTE

interest Index Code (FK)
Floating Note Floor Rate
Floating Note Spread Rate
Floating Note Cap Rate
Floating Note Rate Basis Rate
Floating Note First Reset Rate
Floating Note Time Period Code (FK)

INTEREST INDEX

interest Index Code

Interest Index Time Period Code (FK)
Interest Index Time Period Number
Interest Index Short Name
Interest Index Description
Currency Code (FK)

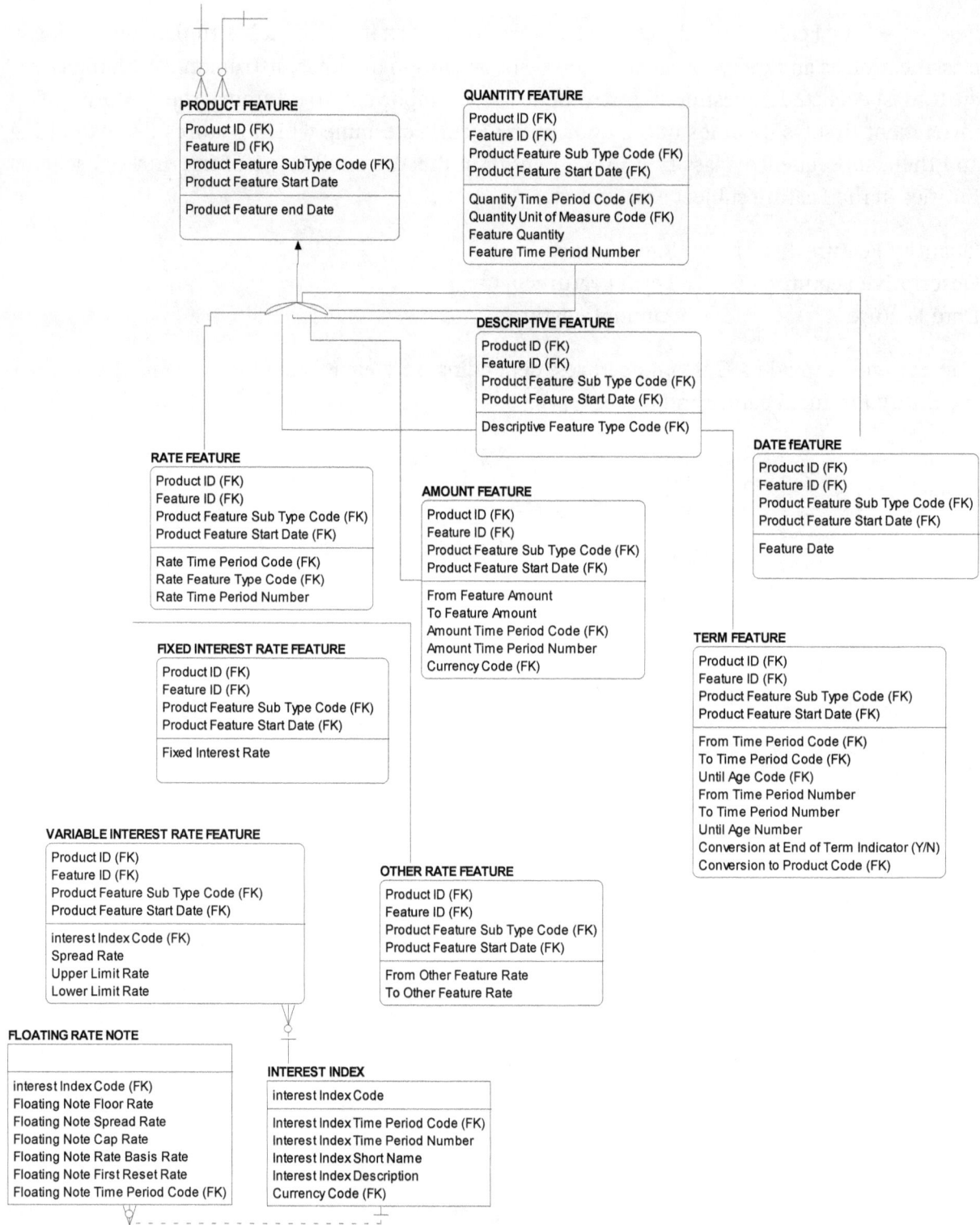

Model 16.08 Feature side of the Investment Product subject area

This concludes our starter modeling for Stock Brokerage/Trade Processing/Investments.

Six

Property, Casualty and Life Insurance

Often, people get property, casualty, and life policies mixed up, and your first two to three business sessions are spent writing the insurance firm's definitions for the several types of insurance they offer.

Property insurance provides financial reimbursement to the owner or renter of a structure and its contents in the event of fire, damage, or theft.

Casualty insurance is a broad category of insurance coverage for individuals, employers, and businesses against loss of property, damage, or other liabilities. Casualty insurance includes vehicle insurance, liability insurance, and theft insurance. Liability losses are losses that occur due to the insured's interactions with others or their property.

Property and Casualty Insurance is classified as either Commercial or Personal.

Life insurance is a contract between an insurance policyholder and an insurance company, where the insurer promises to pay a sum of money in exchange for a premium upon the death of an insured person or after a set period. Life Insurance is sold to an Individual or a Group.

Modeling for insurance starts with the same eight entity Conceptual model as for Banking and Brokerage and expands from there. However, the field of Insurance has an enormous Logical model for these various types of Insurance, in which the terms of the insurance policy are delineated as attributes.

Aspects of the Insurance world which we will not model here include:

- Customer's medical or driving history
- An Insurance Agent or an Insurance firm with many Agents (modeled under the Customer parent or supertype.)
- The Risk and Risk Calculations taken on by Insurance underwriters (separate subject area under the Insurance umbrella)
- Underwriting of insurance policies
- Claims against policies.
- Reinsurance.

You can add them in if your business needs them!

Here are some standard attributes of insurance policies:

Policy Type   Policy Description
Policy Subtype   Policy Identification
Policy Name   Policy Identifier
Policy Start Date time   Policy End Datetime
Policy Payment Frequency   Policy Payment Amount

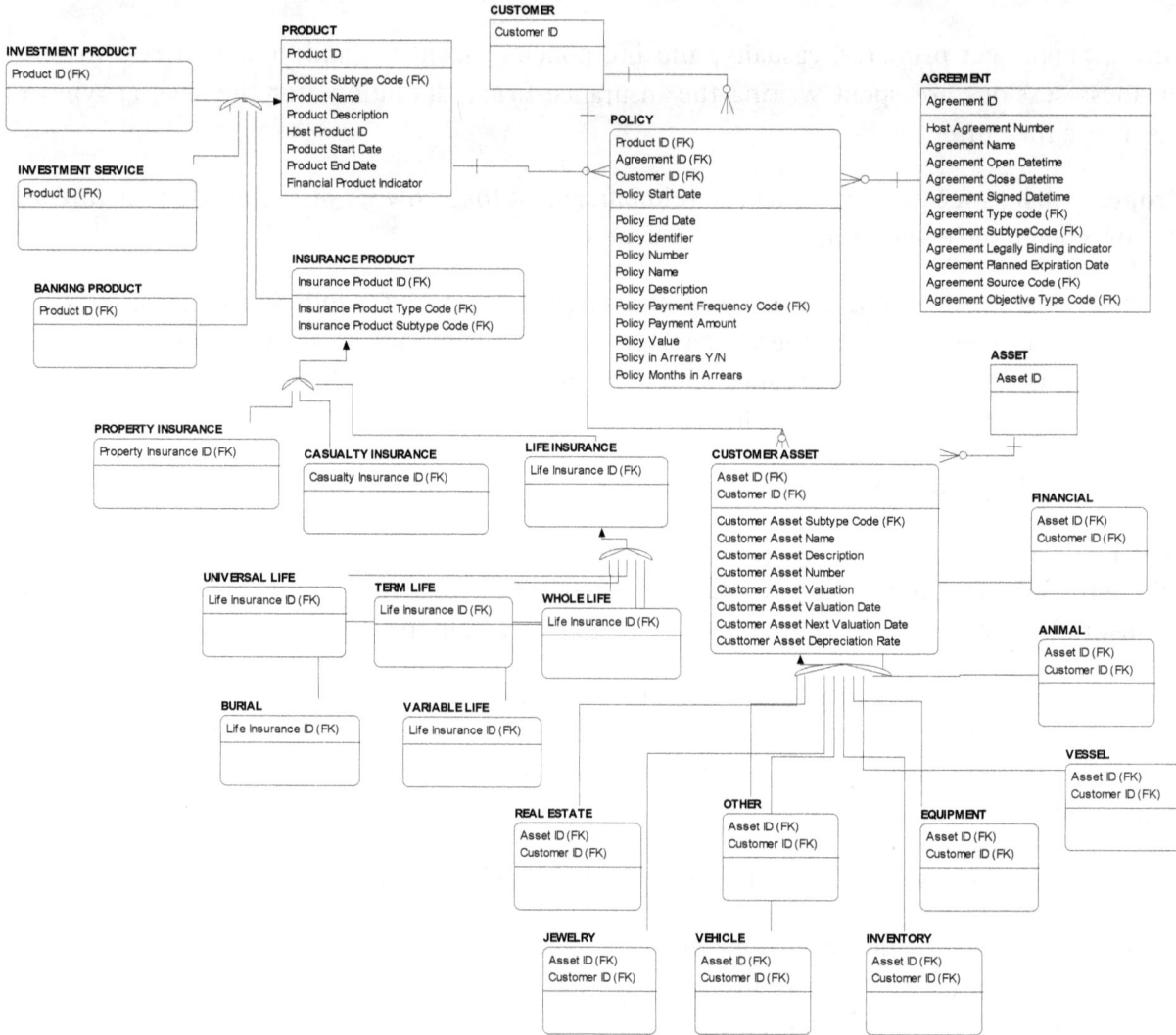

Model 17.0 Insurance Logical ERD

Again, a little difficult to read, so we'll take the left section first, and then the right.

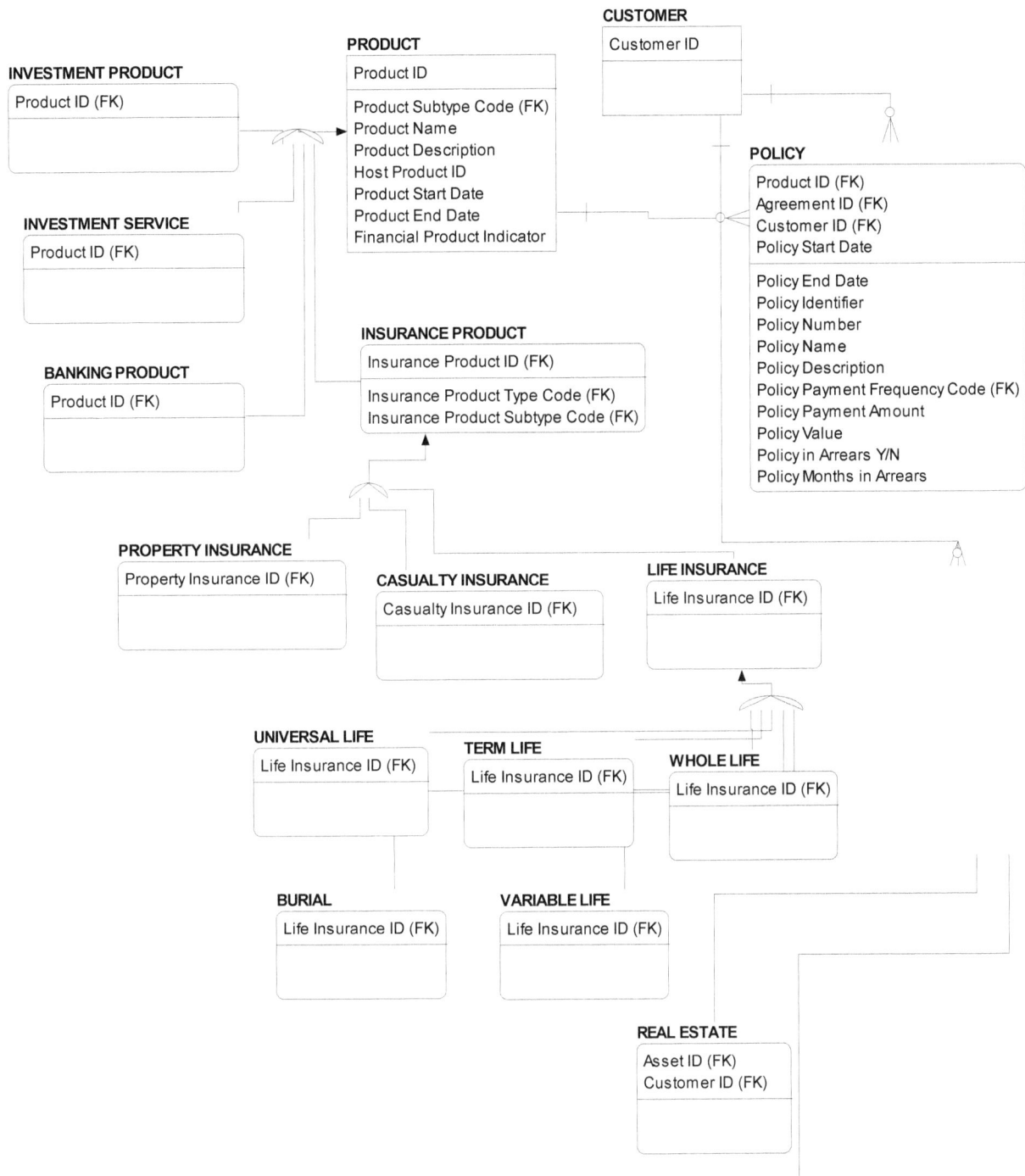

Model 17.01 Left side of Insurance Logical ERD

Here, we see the entity Insurance Product and its three subtypes: Property, Casualty, and Life. Each one of these three is detailed: Life Insurance is detailed as modeled entities while the subtypes of Property and Casualty appear in their respective description fields.

CUSTOMER

Customer ID

POLICY

Product ID (FK)
Agreement ID (FK)
Customer ID (FK)
Policy Start Date

Policy End Date
Policy Identifier
Policy Number
Policy Name
Policy Description
Policy Payment Frequency Code (FK)
Policy Payment Amount
Policy Value
Policy in Arrears Y/N
Policy Months in Arrears

AGREEMENT

Agreement ID

Host Agreement Number
Agreement Name
Agreement Open Datetime
Agreement Close Datetime
Agreement Signed Datetime
Agreement Type code (FK)
Agreement SubtypeCode (FK)
Agreement Legally Binding indicator
Agreement Planned Expiration Date
Agreement Source Code (FK)
Agreement Objective Type Code (FK)

INSURANCE PRODUCT

Insurance Product ID (FK)

Insurance Product Type Code (FK)
Insurance Product Subtype Code (FK)

ASSET

Asset ID

CASUALTY INSURANCE

Casualty Insurance ID (FK)

LIFE INSURANCE

Life Insurance ID (FK)

CUSTOMER ASSET

Asset ID (FK)
Customer ID (FK)

Customer Asset Subtype Code (FK)
Customer Asset Name
Customer Asset Description
Customer Asset Number
Customer Asset Valuation
Customer Asset Valuation Date
Customer Asset Next Valuation Date
Custtomer Asset Depreciation Rate

FINANCIAL

Asset ID (FK)
Customer ID (FK)

TERM LIFE

Life Insurance ID (FK)

WHOLE LIFE

Life Insurance ID (FK)

ANIMAL

Asset ID (FK)
Customer ID (FK)

VARIABLE LIFE

Life Insurance ID (FK)

VESSEL

Asset ID (FK)
Customer ID (FK)

REAL ESTATE

Asset ID (FK)
Customer ID (FK)

OTHER

Asset ID (FK)
Customer ID (FK)

EQUIPMENT

Asset ID (FK)
Customer ID (FK)

JEWELRY

Asset ID (FK)
Customer ID (FK)

VEHICLE

Asset ID (FK)
Customer ID (FK)

INVENTORY

Asset ID (FK)
Customer ID (FK)

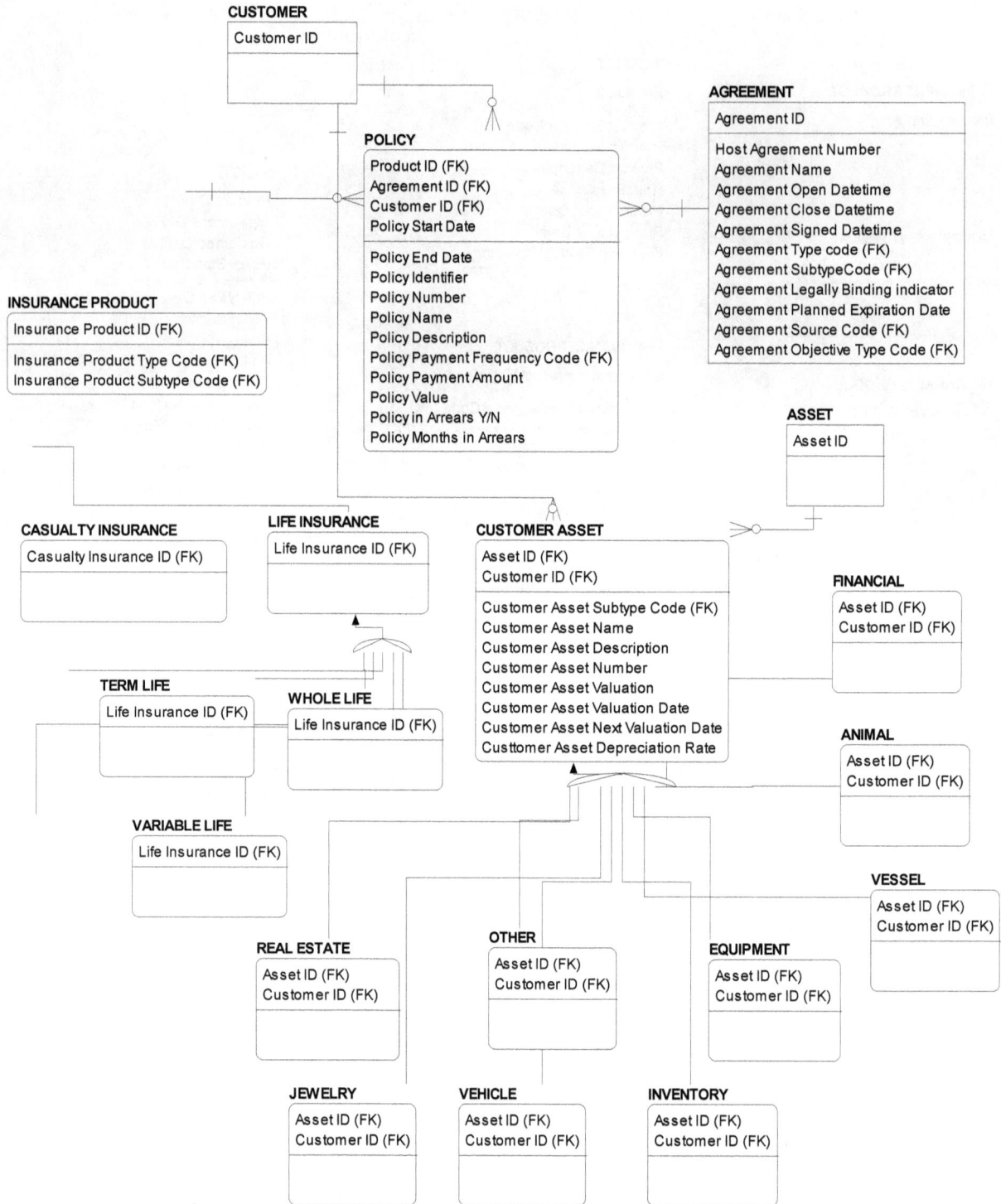

Model 17.02 Right side of Insurance Logical ERD

Here we see the initial delineation of Customer Agreement, which is the entity Policy, with the many subtypes of Assets for which the Policy could cover.

SEVEN

Capital and Finance

There are three concepts a Modeler has to understand to model Finance: General Ledger, Journal, and Chart of Accounts:

- A **General Ledger** is the main accounting record for a business or organization. It is a set of numbered accounts a business uses to keep track of its financial transactions and prepare financial reports. Each account is a unique record summarizing a specific type of asset, liability, equity, revenue, or expense.

- A **Journal** is a running record of all of a business's financial transactions. It is used to reconcile accounts and is transferred to other accounting records, such as the general ledger. The journal states the date of a transaction, which accounts were affected, and the dollar amounts, usually in a double-entry bookkeeping method.

- **A Chart of Accounts** is an index of all financial accounts in a company's general ledger. In short, it is an organizational tool that lists by category and line item all of the financial transactions a company conducts during a specific accounting period.

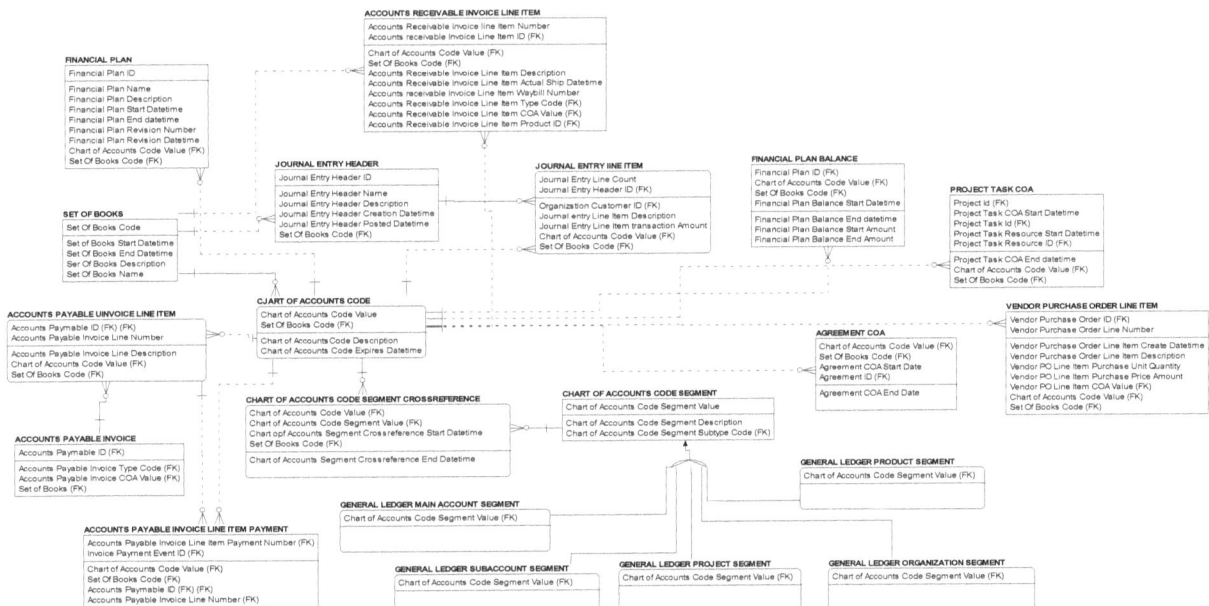

Model 18.0 Capital and Finance Logical ERD for Journal and Chart of Accounts

Again, it's too small to read, so we'll split it into two sections, left and right.

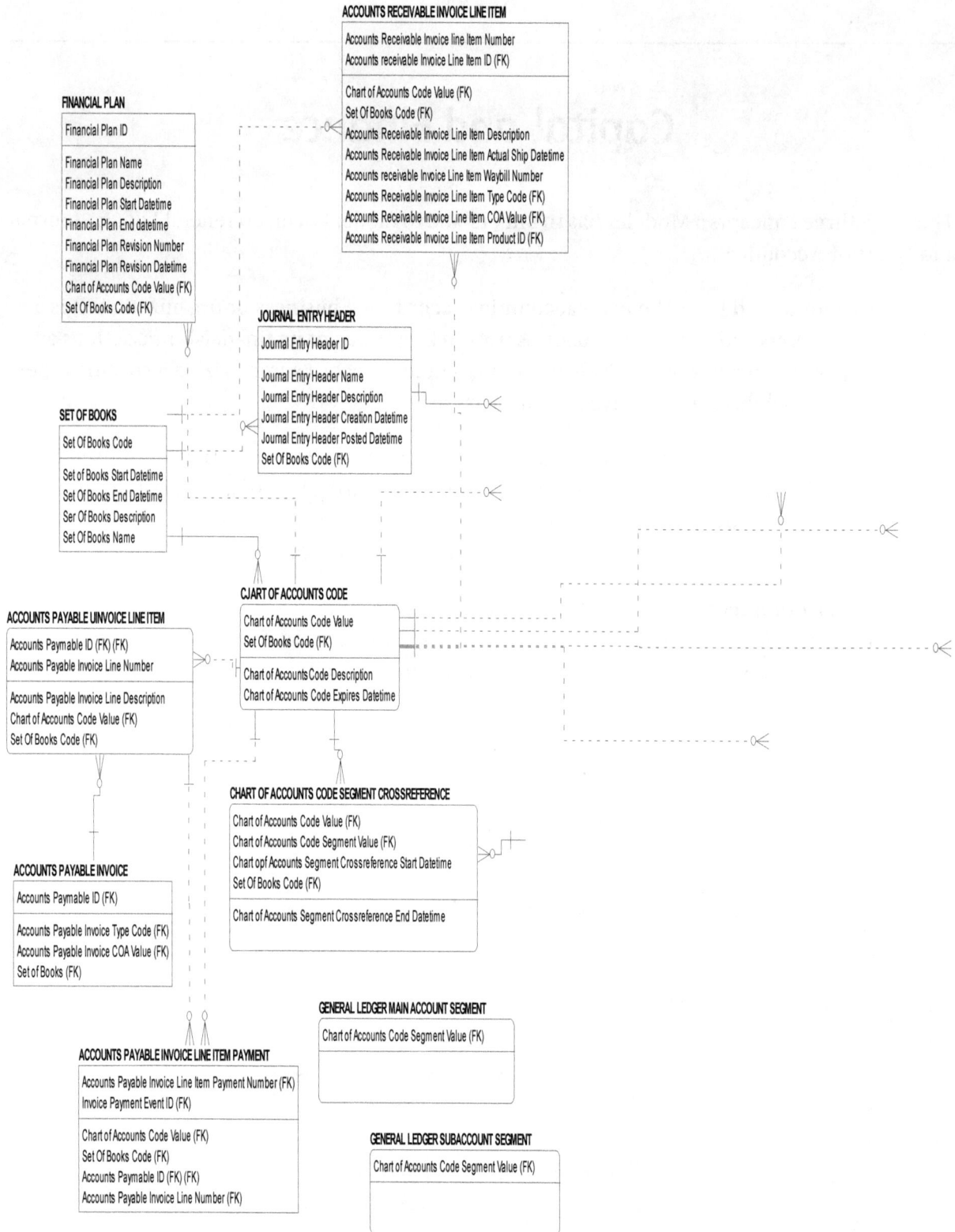

ACCOUNTS RECEIVABLE INVOICE LINE ITEM

Accounts Receivable Invoice line Item Number
Accounts receivable Invoice Line Item ID (FK)

Chart of Accounts Code Value (FK)
Set Of Books Code (FK)
Accounts Receivable Invoice Line Item Description
Accounts Receivable Invoice Line Item Actual Ship Datetime
Accounts receivable Invoice Line Item Waybill Number
Accounts receivable Invoice Line Item Type Code (FK)
Accounts Receivable Invoice Line Item COA Value (FK)
Accounts Receivable Invoice Line Item Product ID (FK)

FINANCIAL PLAN

Financial Plan ID

Financial Plan Name
Financial Plan Description
Financial Plan Start Datetime
Financial Plan End datetime
Financial Plan Revision Number
Financial Plan Revision Datetime
Chart of Accounts Code Value (FK)
Set Of Books Code (FK)

JOURNAL ENTRY HEADER

Journal Entry Header ID

Journal Entry Header Name
Journal Entry Header Description
Journal Entry Header Creation Datetime
Journal Entry Header Posted Datetime
Set Of Books Code (FK)

SET OF BOOKS

Set Of Books Code

Set of Books Start Datetime
Set Of Books End Datetime
Ser Of Books Description
Set Of Books Name

CJART OF ACCOUNTS CODE

Chart of Accounts Code Value
Set Of Books Code (FK)

Chart of Accounts Code Description
Chart of Accounts Code Expires Datetime

ACCOUNTS PAYABLE UINVOICE LINE ITEM

Accounts Paymable ID (FK) (FK)
Accounts Payable Invoice Line Number

Accounts Payable Invoice Line Description
Chart of Accounts Code Value (FK)
Set Of Books Code (FK)

CHART OF ACCOUNTS CODE SEGMENT CROSSREFERENCE

Chart of Accounts Code Value (FK)
Chart of Accounts Code Segment Value (FK)
Chart opf Accounts Segment Crossreference Start Datetime
Set Of Books Code (FK)

Chart of Accounts Segment Crossreference End Datetime

ACCOUNTS PAYABLE INVOICE

Accounts Paymable ID (FK)

Accounts Payable Invoice Type Code (FK)
Accounts Payable Invoice COA Value (FK)
Set of Books (FK)

GENERAL LEDGER MAIN ACCOUNT SEGMENT

Chart of Accounts Code Segment Value (FK)

GENERAL LEDGER SUBACCOUNT SEGMENT

Chart of Accounts Code Segment Value (FK)

ACCOUNTS PAYABLE INVOICE LINE ITEM PAYMENT

Accounts Payable Invoice Line Item Payment Number (FK)
Invoice Payment Event ID (FK)

Chart of Accounts Code Value (FK)
Set Of Books Code (FK)
Accounts Paymable ID (FK) (FK)
Accounts Payable Invoice Line Number (FK)

Left side of Model 18.01 Journal and Chart of Accounts

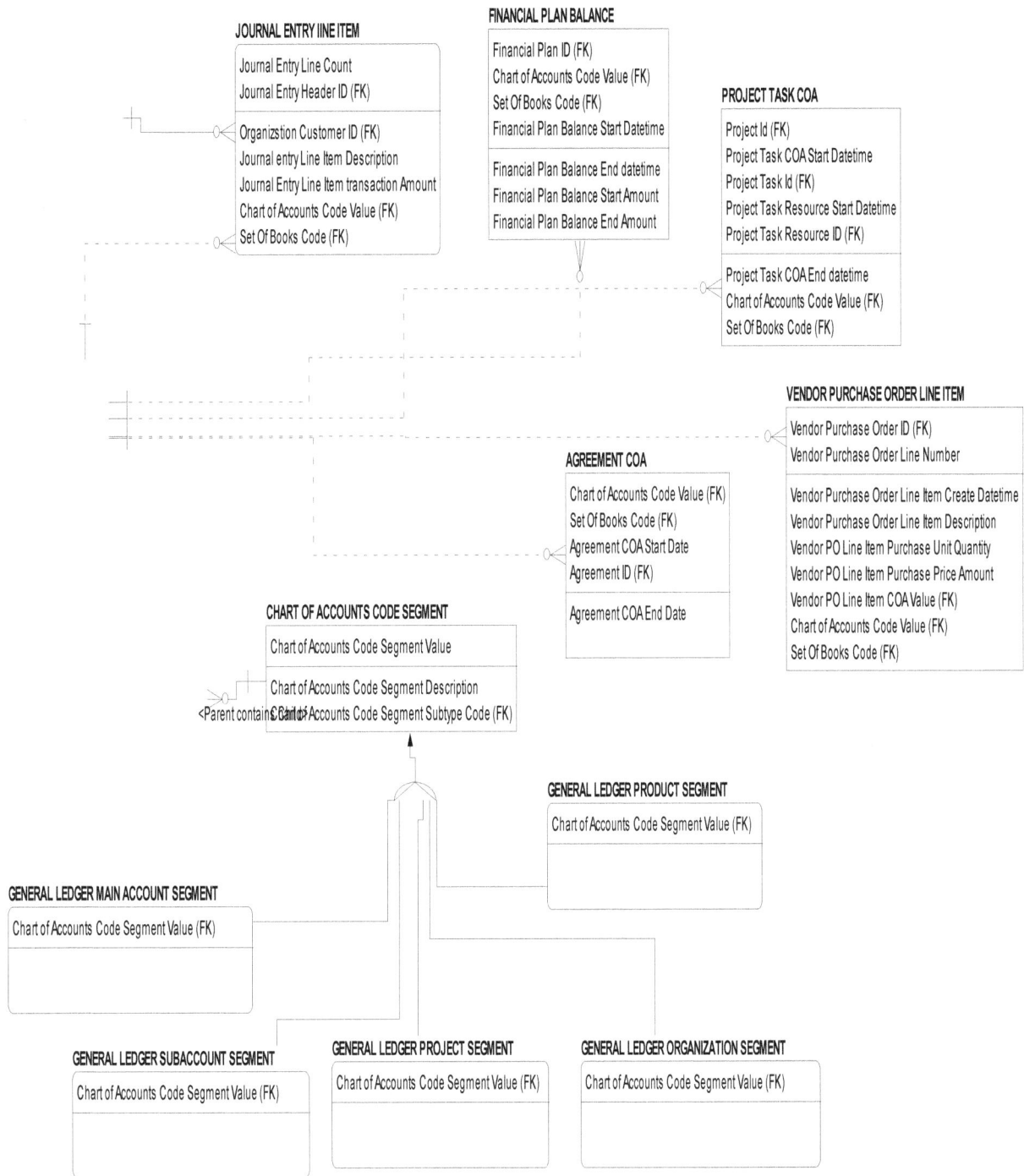

Right side of Model 18.02 **Journal and Chart of Accounts**

A stand-alone piece of our Capital and Finance model is the General Ledger of the Firm. It is fairly straightforward:

GENERAL LEDGER MAIN ACCOUNT

General Ledger Account Value

General Ledger Account Name
general Ledger Account Description
General Ledger Account Start Datetime
General Ledger Account End Datetime
General Ledger Main Account Category Code (FK)
Parent General Ledger Main Account Name (FK)
General Ledger Main Account External Indicator Y/N

BALANCE SHEET MAIN ACCOUNT

General Ledger Account Value (FK)

Balance Sheet General Ledger Main Account Code (FK)
Balance Sheet Code (FK)

INCOME STATEMENT GENERAL LEDGER MAIN ACCOUNT

General Ledger Account Value (FK)

Income Statement General Ledger Main Account Subtype Code (FK)

ASSET ACCOUNT

General Ledger Account Value (FK)

Asset Account Subtype Code (FK)

EQUITY ACCOUNT

General Ledger Account Value (FK)

Equity Account Subtype Code (FK)

EXPENSE ACCOUNT

General Ledger Account Value (FK)

Expense Account Subtype Code (FK)

REVENUE ACCOUNT

General Ledger Account Value (FK)

revenue Account Subtype Code (FK)

LIABILITY ACCOUNT

General Ledger Account Value (FK)

ILiability Account Subtype Code (FK)

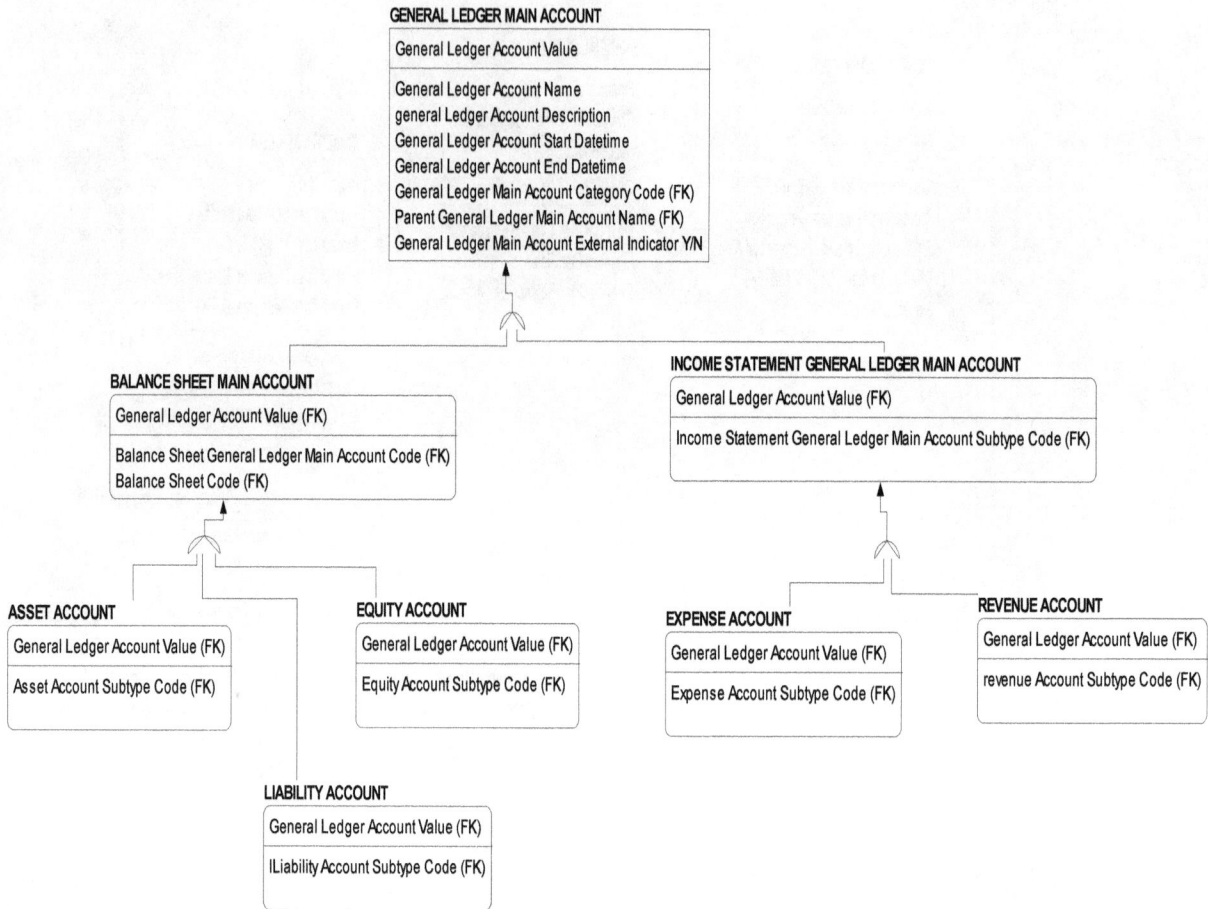

Model 18.03 General Ledger in Capital and Finance

This concludes our introduction to financial Logical modeling. When are you done? When is the Logical Model complete? It is complete when your business users can trace every task in their daily, weekly, monthly, and annual work activities, and understand how to report on them. .

When you are nearing the end of Logical modeling, add your Physical DBAs to your model reviews. Familiarize them with the business behind the completed Logical Model and the model's structure itself.

EIGHT

Physical Data Models

Now is the time for all good Modelers to pick their heads up and look at the target database. Well, not really. After all, during your Logical modeling, you have been using a data set to specify data types and lengths, which was selected for your target server or mainframe, right?

If your target server is a powerful Teradata, Oracle, or IBM configuration, you may need to simply add housekeeping attributes to each entity and run it through your modeling tool to create DDL and Tables —essentially prepping the Logical model to run as is.

What do we mean by housekeeping attributes? We are obsessed with the business in Logical modeling—how it operates and the data it stores. We try to ignore source systems, source data, tracking (non-business) timestamps, the timestamp for when it was last modified, who modified it (employee's ID), etc. However, for a database to function properly/in a timely fashion, we must consider these facts, which are part of Physical modeling.

For this type of Physical modeling, there are usually four to ten attributes appended to the bottom of each table to facilitate operations. These housekeeping attributes may include a timestamp for each time data is added to or deleted from a table, a code for each source of the data (particularly if there is more than one source), the ID of the person modifying the data, etc.

Alternatively, if your target is not one of the really powerful servers, you must denormalize your Logical model, which has been, up until now, be in Third Normal Form (3NF). This means collapsing, merging, or integrating related tables together.

The trick to a successful denormalization is to merge tables that are actually related. For example, don't merge Customer and Product! Denormalization is a bit of an art form.

Take your Logical model as is, add the housekeeping attributes, create DDL, and run it in a partitioned section of production, or use a development instance populated at regular intervals with data from production. Time the run programmatically. Then, take the same section of your Logical Model, denormalize it, add housekeeping attributes, create DDL, and run this test case in the same area of production or development. Time this programmatically. Do you see an improvement? If yes, keep going! If not, try test runs on a larger section of your Logical Model to see if you get better results in production or development.

CUSTOMER CREDIT RATING

Customer Credit Rating ID
Customer ID (FK)

Customer Credit Rating
Customer Credit Rating Datetime
Credit Reporting Agency Code (FK)

CUSTOMER ROLE

Customer Role ID

Customer Role Description
Customer Role Type Code
Customer Role Start Date
Customer Role End Date
Role Legal Appointment Document

CUSTOMER ASSET

Customer Asset ID
Customer ID (FK)

Customer Asset Description
Customer Asset Type Code
Customer Asset Value

CUSTOMER IDENTIFICATION

Customer Identification ID (FK)
Issuing Party ID
Customer Identification Type Code (FK)
Customer ID Start Date

Customer Id End Date
Customer Identification Alphanumeric

ROLE SPECIAL INSTRUCTION

Customer Role ID (FK)
Role Special Instruction ID

Role Special Instruction Description
Role Special Instruction From Date
Role Special Instruction To Date

CUSTOMER RELATED

Customer ID (FK)
Customer Role ID (FK)
Customer Related ID (FK)
Customer Related Role Code (FK)
Customer Related Start Date

Customer Related End Date
Customer Structure Type (FK)
Customer Related Reason Code (FK)
Customer Related Status Type Code (FK)

CUSTOMER

Customer ID

Customer Description
Customer Start Date
Customer End Date
Customer Subtype Code (FK)
Customer Type Code (FK)
Customer Initial Data Source Type Code (FK)
GDPR/CCPA Eligible YN
SEC Classification ID (FK)

STATUS

Status ID

Status Code
Status Description

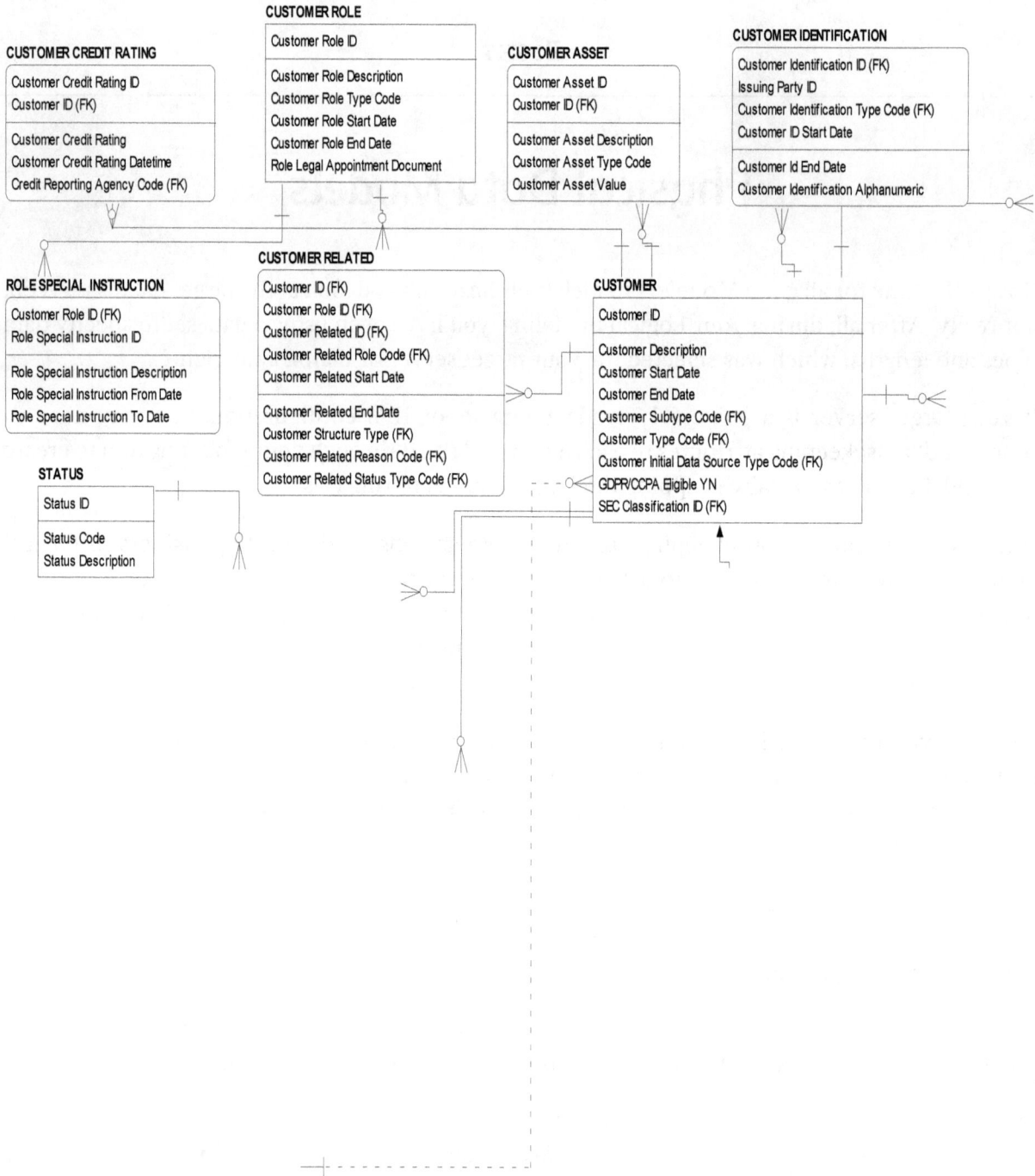

Here's an example: Let's look at the top part of the Customer Logical model:

Ok, now denormalized to a certain degree:

CUSTOMER ROLE

Customer Role ID
Customer Role Description Customer Role Type Code (FK) Customer Role Start Date Customer Role End date Role Legal appointment document Role Special Instruction Description Role Special Instruction From Date Role Special Instruction To Date

CUSTOMER ASSET

Customer ID (FK) Customer asset ID
Customer Asset Description Customer Asset type Code Customer Asset Value

CUSTOMER RELATED

Customer Role ID (FK) Custome Related ID (FK) Customer related Start Date Customer ID (FK) Customer Related Role Code (FK) (FK)
Customer Related End Date Customer Structure Type (FK) Customer Related Reasion Code (FK) Customer related Status type Code (FK)

CUSTOMER

Customer ID
Customer Full Name Customer Description Customer Start Date Customer End Date Customer Subtype Code (FK) Customer Type Code (FK) Customer Initial Data Source Type Code (FK) GDPR/CCPA Eligible YN Customer ID Issuing Party (FK) Customer Identification Type Code (FK) Customer Identification Start Date Customer Identification End Date Customer Identification Alphanumeric Customer Credit Rating Customer Credit Rating Datetime Customer Credit Reporting Agency Code (FK)

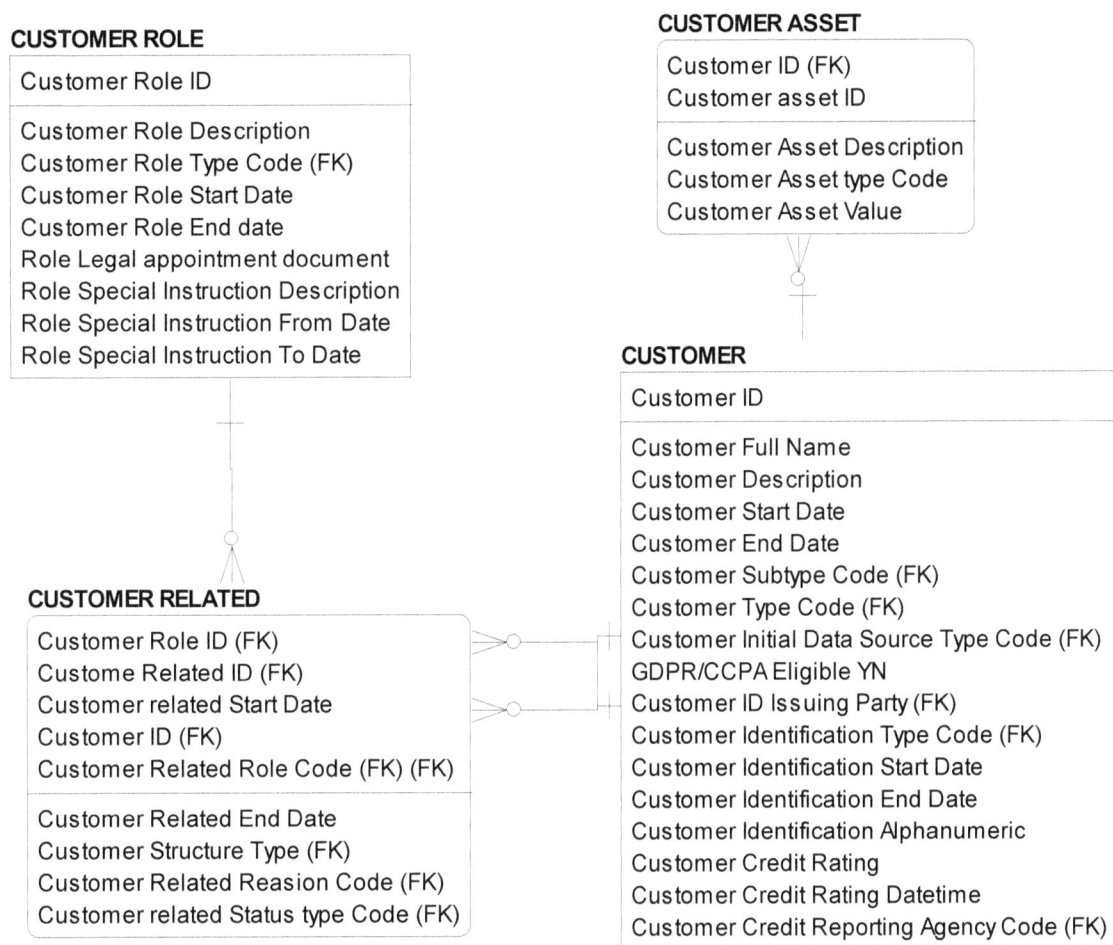

Model 19.0 Denormalized partial Customer Logical into a Physical ERD

To create DDL, add the necessary housekeeping attributes to the bottom of each table and initialize DDL creation in your modeling tool!

Create your entire Physical ERD by either denormalizing your Logical and adding the necessary housekeeping attributes or by adding the housekeeping attributes to your Logical Model for a powerful server. Conduct a model review with the DBAs and Senior Management.

Create the first cut of DDL and review it with your DBAs.

Announce, in documentation, that you are done and available to help the process in a secondary fashion. Make every effort to be available to the business people and the DBAs for consultations, even if your next assignment has taken off.

Reporting / Data Warehouse / Star Schema

Um, how about reporting? Of course, you can generate reports using your previous OLTP design. However, running reports from a Data Warehouse (DW) design might be easier. A data warehouse design consists of facts and dimensions in a star schema configuration.

For example:

CUSTOMER

Customer ID

TRANSACTION

Transaction ID

CUSTOMER ASSET

Customer Asset ID

PRODUCT

Product ID

Sales Number

Customer ID (FK)
Transaction ID (FK)
Datetime ID (FK)
Product ID (FK)
Customer Asset ID (FK)
Sales Number
Revenue Amount
High Volume Day
Low Volume Day
Value of Assets as Collateral
Number of Assets Held as Collateral
Risk Calculation

DATETIME

Datetime ID
Date
Datetime

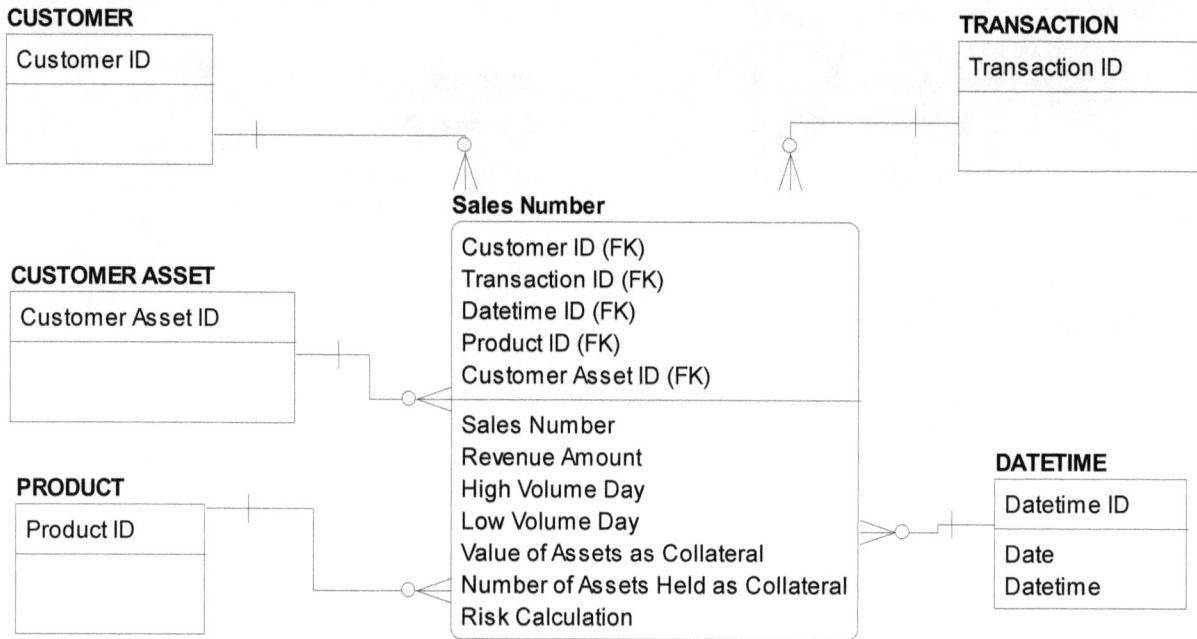

Model 20.0 High Level Data Warehouse Sample

In real life, data warehouses may contain hundreds of dimension tables and (usually) more than one fact table, but that is your next adventure!

Definitions

The source of each definition is in the parentheses () at the end of each definition. (CLF) is a definition provided by the Author. Other sources are given as their website, e.g. (SEC.gov, Investopedia.com, etc.).

- **Account** – A record in virtual and/or Physical form of a specific type of transactions between two legal entities, usually based upon an initial agreement. Examples include: bank accounts, brokerage accounts. Note: An Agreement may result in the establishment of several different types of Accounts, but an Account belongs to one Agreement (CLF)

- **Accounts Payable Invoice** – A bill or invoice of the money owed to a vendor or supplier for goods or services purchased on credit; the obligations incurred by a company during its operations that remain due and must be paid in the short term. (Google.com)

- **Accounts Payable Invoice Line Item** – A single line of information on an Accounts Payable Invoice, usually containing a line identifier, a short description of the item, the quantity and the amount of money due. (CLF)

- **Accounts Payable Invoice Line Item Payment** – Information about the payment for a line item on the invoice. (CLF)

- **Accounts Receivable Invoice Line Item** - A time-stamped commercial document with important information about a customer's purchase. Each item purchased is represented in a separate line on the invoice. It serves as a record of the transaction and outlines all the details related to the sale, including items purchased, quantities, prices, payment terms, and due dates. (Google.com)

- **Agreement** – A contract to perform the sale or usage of a Product and/or the delivery of a service between two or more legal entities. Examples include: an insurance policy, a contract with a financial advisor, credit card usage terms, etc. (CLF)

- **Agreement COA (Chart of Accounts)** – This entity ties the underlying agreement to its chart of accounts and to a set of books. (CLF)

- **Alternative Investment** – Any investment outside of the traditional holdings of stock, bonds and cash. Alternative investments may include real estate, hedge funds, private credit, and/or luxury investments such as rare whiskeys, jewelry, etc. (CLF)

- **Amount Feature** – The money or value associated with a particular financial instrument or transaction, and the time period it is in effect. Examples include: $1000.00 (amount of a government bond), $5,000.00 (amount/ today's value of 100 shares of a stock whose unit price is $50.00) (CLF)

- **Asset** – Property owned by a person or company regarded as having value and available to meet debts, commitments or legacies. (Dictionary.com)

- **Asset Account** – A General Ledger account used to sort and store the debit and credit amounts from a company's transactions involving the company's resources. (AccountingCoach.com)

- **Asset-backed Security** – A type of financial investment that is collateralized by an underlying pool of assets – usually ones that generate a cash flow from debt, such as loans, leases, credit card debt or receivables. (Google.com)

- **Balance Sheet Main Account** - A financial statement that contains details of a company's assets or liabilities at a specific point in time. It is one of the three core financial statements (income statement and cash flow statement being the other two) used for evaluating the performance of a business. (Google.com)

- **Banking Product** – A product purchased from a bank with the intent to grow the product and/or receive a return, such as interest. (CLF)

- **Bond** – A fixed income instrument and investment product in which individuals lend money to a company or a government at a certain interest rate for an amount. (Investopedia.com)

- **Bond Conversion Schedule** – A schedule for changing a bond into equity shares. The schedule is published to bond-holders when the conversion steps are determined. The number of shares that a bond can be converted into depends upon the conversion ratio, while the conversion price determines the cost per share. (Google.com)

- **Burial or Burial Insurance** – Burial insurance, also known as funeral or final expense insurance, is a type of whole life insurance policy designed to cover one's funeral, burial and other end-of-life expenses. (Google.com)

- **Calendar** – A chart or series of pages showing the days, weeks, and months of a particular year or giving seasonal information. (Google)

- **Campaign** – A strategic sequence of steps and activities designed to promote a financial firm's products and/or services with the goal of increasing sales and/or utilization. (CLF)

- **Cash Equivalents** – Cash Equivalents include bank accounts and some types of marketable securities such as commercial paper and short term government bonds, which can be turned into cash on short notice. (Google.com)

- **Casualty Insurance** – A broad category of insurance coverage against loss of property, damage or other liabilities. (Investopedia.com)

- **Certificate of Deposit** (CD) - A type of savings account offered by a Bank or a Credit Union. Funds are deposited for a specific length of time; withdrawal of the CD prior to its end date results in a withdrawal fine or fee. (Consumer Financial Protection Bureau)

- **Channel** – The method by which information is transmitted. Example: Superbowl game and advertisements have the channel of television. (CLF + SH)

- **Chart of Accounts Code – (COA)** A financial organizational tool that provides a complete listing, by category and line item, of every account in the General Ledger of a company during a specific accounting period. Used to organize finances and give investors and shareholders a clearer view of the company's financial health. (Investopedia.com)

  - **Attribute: COA Code Value** – A code assigned by the business to the various categories which Assets and Liabilities are broken down into. For example: categories of Assets may include 01 Cash, 02 Savings Account, 03 Petty Cash Balance, 04 Accounts Receivable, 05 Undeposited funds, etc. (Investopedia.com)
  - **Attribute: Set of Books Code** - A set of books determines the functional currency, account structure, and accounting calendar for each company or group of companies. If it is necessary to report on a Firm's account balances in multiple currencies, one additional set of books for each reporting currency should be set up. (Google.com)

- **Chart of Accounts Code Segment** – Segments are components of an account string. Each segment has a name and defined length, usually 6 digits. Example: (Ohio University)

Segment Value	Account Type
Balance Sheet	
1XXXXX	Asset Codes
2XXXXX	Liability Codes
3XXXXX	Fund Balance Codes
Income Statement	
4XXXXX	Revenue Codes
6XXXXX	Funding Transfer Codes
7XXXXX	Expense Codes
8XXXXX	Investment Transfers

- **Chart of Accounts Segment Cross Reference** – The cross reference between Chart of Accounts Code and the Chart of Accounts Code Segment, especially for Firms which are designing additional segments. (Ohio University)

- **Commercial Paper** – Short term promissory notes issued by companies. (Dictionary.com)

- **Commodity** – A Physical item, such as gold or silver, that possesses intrinsic value. (Yieldstreet.com)

- **Commodity Option** – A derivative contract which enables the buyer (holder or owner) of the instrument the right to buy or sell the underlying futures. (Google.com)

- **Common Stock** – A class of stock that represents equity ownership in a corporation. (Cornell Law School)

- **Convertible Bond** – A fixed-income debt security that pays interest but can be converted into shares of common stock or equity shares. (Investopedia.com)

- **Corporate Bond** – An investment in the debt of a business, and are a common way for a Firm to raise debt capital. (Investopedia.com)

- **Corporate Card** – A child of Credit Card Agreement; a credit card issued to officers of a corporation, with specific terms of usage. (CLF)

- **Country/ Currency** – One of the Reference Entities, not shown in every model, but added when necessary. This Reference Entity contains a valid chart(s) of nation names, nation abbreviations (ISO 2- and 3-character), the associated currency (monetary form) and valid monetary abbreviations, including ISO codes, in accordance with ISO 4217. (CLF + ISO 4217)

- **Credit Agreement** – A child of Financial Agreement; a contract to extend credit (a line of credit amount) to a legal entity. (CLF)

- **Credit Card Agreement** – A child of Loan Agreement; a contract to provide credit when a credit card is presented to a vendor. Examples include: Mastercard agreement, Visa credit card agreement, etc.

- **Credit Rating** - An estimate of the ability of a person or an organization to fulfill their financial commitments, based on previous dealings. For individuals, the three most utilized credit rating agencies are Transunion, Equifax and Experian. For companies, the most utilized credit reporting agencies are: Equifax, Experian and Dun & Bradstreet. (Investopedia.com)

- **Credit Security** – A variety of tests administered to a client's financial services records and/or internal accounts to determine the safety of doing business with this customer, including KYC ("Know Your Customer" regulation) tests, and other mandated testing. (CLF)

- **Currency Contract** – A subtype of Investment Product; any futures contract or option thereon providing for the delivery or receipt at a future date of a specified amount of a traded currency at a specified price and delivery point, or any other futures contract or option thereon approved for trading by U.S. citizens. (lawinsider.com)

- **Currency Option** – A subtype of Option; a currency option (also known as a forex option) is a contract that gives the buyer the right, but not the obligation, to buy or sell a certain currency at a specified exchange rate on or before a specified date. For this right, a premium is paid to the seller. (Investopedia.com)

- **CUSIP Product Identifier** – A subtype of Product Identification; CUSIP stands for Committee on Uniform Securities Identification Procedures. A CUSIP number identifies most financial instruments, including: stocks of all registered U.S. and Canadian companies, commercial paper, and U.S. government and municipal bonds. (Google.com)

- **Customer** – A legal entity with the authority to sign contracts and transact business in said contracts; a person over the age of 18 or 21 (depending upon the State or Country); a Corporation, a Company (that has filed a DBA "Doing Business As"); a Trust or other legal entity recognized by the Courts. (CLF)

- o **Attribute:** GDPR/CCPA Eligible (Y/N) - If the customer is a citizen of a European country, they are subject to GDPR regulations (Y); If the customer is a U.S. citizen and a resident of California, they are subject to CCPA regulations (Y); otherwise, (N).

- **Customer Asset** – An item of value owned by a customer. Examples include: a home, a building, funded accounts at various firms, cars, boats, jewelry, etc. (CLF)

- **Customer Credit Rating** – An evaluation of the credit risk of a prospective debtor (an individual, business, company or government) predicting their ability to pay back the debt and implicit forecast of the likelihood of the debtor defaulting. (Wikipedia.com)

- **Customer Event** – An occurrence of importance to a Customer, which may or may not have an impact on the Customer's assets or accounts, but is important enough for a financial advisor to note. Examples include: the birth of a child, the retirement of a Customer or Customer's spouse. (CLF)

- **Customer Financial Document/ KYC** – Information about a company's or an individual's monetary positions or holdings, not found in the Agreement or Account, and of interest to the firm, person or household. This entity may include KYC ("Know Your Customer") questions and answers or they may be normalized into a separate entity. (CLF)

- **Customer Financial Information** – Historical information of all of the Customer's transactions with the Firm, including any external financial information, which may be of importance in making lending decisions. (CLF)

- **Customer Identification** – Each customer whether they are an individual or a business has one or more identification strings. These may be a Social Security Number, a Tax Identification number or other identification number. (CLF)

- **Customer/Location** – A resolution of the many-to-many relationship between Customer and Location. The primary location or home address of where the Customer lives, receives mail, and/or works. The primary address of a Customer which is a business or a corporation. Alternate address information is put in additional records here. Additional records may include a second home, a branch office address, or other pertinent customer locations. (CLF)

- **Customer/Mortgage/Loan** – contains the details of a mortgage or loan which the Customer has signed, including the address of the property, if a mortgage, the amount borrowed, and comparable value of similar properties, if a mortgage.

- **Customer/Product** – This entity resolves the many-to-many relationship between Customer and Product. It specifies exactly which product(s) have been purchased by which Customers. (CLF)

- **Customer Related** – a non-identifying relationship between two entities representing the fact that one company can own another company, or that a parent (Mother or Father) is related to a child (Daughter or Son), i.e. familial relationships, corporate reporting relationships, etc. (CLF)

- **Customer Role** – Not the salutation, but the role or activity that a Customer plays in a family or a company. Examples include: granddaughter, son, Treasurer, Corporate Secretary, etc. (CLF)

- **Customer Salutation** – An expression of greeting or courtesy. Examples include: Ms., Dr., Mr., Mrs., etc. (CLF)

- **Customer Status** – The specific state of a particular customer's account; see Status for codes. (CLF)

- **Date Feature** – A calendar event associated with a particular Financial Instrument. Examples include: Option expiration date, settlement date, etc. (CLF)

- **Datetime** – A set of characters usually in a prescribed format used to express the year, the month, the day of the month, the hour of the day, the minutes of the hour, and the time zone. (Google)

- **Derivative** – A subtype of Investment Product; an arrangement or instrument (such as a future, option, or warrant) whose value derives from and is dependent on the value of an underlying asset. (Dictionary.com)

- **Descriptive Feature** – Text, giving the name of the Financial Instrument, and (optionally) information about the Financial Instrument. For example: Amtrak Railway Bond, to provide funding for the extension of railroad service to northern Maine. (CLF)

- **Equipment** – a subtype of Customer Asset; the set of tools, clothing, etc., needed for a particular activity or purpose. (dictionary.cambridge.org)

- **Equity** - An ownership interest in property that may be offset by debts or other liabilities. Equity is measured for accounting purposes by subtracting liabilities from the value of the assets owned. (Wikipedia.com)

- **Equity Account** – In a General Ledger, the remaining value of an owner's interest in a company after subtracting all liabilities from total assets; the amount the owner or shareholders would get back if the business paid off all its debt and liquidated all its assets. (Google.com)

- **Event** – An occurrence of importance to the business and may result in a change to a customer's assets or account. An event may also be of importance to the Firm itself, whether or not it affects customer's assets, such as a change in management structure. (CLF)

- **Exchange** – A marketplace for the buying and selling of financial instruments. Examples include: the New York Stock Exchange (NYSE) and the National Association of Securities Dealers Automated Quotation (NASDAQ) (CLF)

- **Exchange Traded Funds, ETF** – ETFs are similar to mutual funds in that they invest in a basket of securities, such as stocks, bonds, or other asset classes. but unlike mutual funds and similar to a stock, ETFs can be traded whenever the markets are open. (ishares.com)

- **Expense Account** – In the General Ledger, records of the amount a company spends on day-to-day costs during a given accounting period. These accounts exist for a set period of time - a month, quarter, or year - and then new accounts are created for each new period. (Google.com)

- **Family Card** – a child of Credit Card Agreement, issued to members of a family household. It may or may not have specific terms of usage. (CLF)

- **Feature** – A distinctive contributor or an aspect of a Financial Instrument; a component of a Financial Instrument. Examples include: interest rate, dividend schedule, term, quantity, amount, etc. (CLF)

- **Financial** – A subtype of Customer Asset; assets of a monetary nature, including cash, stock, bonds, and other monetary holdings and investments. (CLF)

- **Financial Agreement** - A child of Agreement; a contract to perform the sale or usage of a Financial Product and/or the delivery of a financial service between two or more legal entities. Examples include: an insurance policy, a contract with a financial advisor, etc. (CLF)

- **Financial Event** – An occurrence in the market(s) or in business which can potentially effect Customer's assets or accounts. Examples include: a Firm decides to split its stock 3 shares for every 1 share held; a market crash; a bull market which raises the Dow Jones Industrial Average by 1,000 points. (CLF)

- **Financial Plan** - *A document detailing a Firm's or a person's current money situation and long-term monetary goals*, as well as strategies to achieve them. (Investopedia.com)

- **Financial Plan Balance** – A summary (one page) of assets, liabilities and equity. (CLF)

- **Firm** - The term Firm is synonymous with business, company and corporation. (CLF)

- **Firm Organization** – The internal or reporting structure of a business, usually arranged in a tree format, with the President and Senior Officers at the top of the tree and mid- to lower level officers below. (CLF)

- **Fixed Interest Rate** – An interest rate (see Rate Feature) that never changes its value. (CLF)

- **Fixed Interest Rate Feature** – A subtype of Rate Feature; a feature of a financial instrument assigned at its inception, wherein the interest rate does not change. (CLF)

- **Floating Rate Note** – A fixed income security that pays a coupon (interest) determined by a reference rate which resets periodically. (SEC.gov)

- **Forward Contract** – A customized contract between two parties to buy or sell an asset at a specified price on a future date. Used for hedging. (SEC.gov)

- **Future Option** – An option on a futures contract gives the holder the right, but not the obligation, to buy or sell a specific futures contract at a strike price on or before the option's expiration date. These work similarly to stock options, but differ in that the underlying security is a futures contract. (Investopedia.com)

- **Futures Contract** – An agreement traded on an organized exchange to buy or sell assets especially commodities or shares at a fixed price, but to be delivered and paid for later. (Dictionary.com)

- **General Ledger** – General Ledger accounts are account numbers used to categorize types of financial transactions. All primary asset accounts begin with the number 1; all liabilities begin with the number 2; the order of assets are assets, liabilities, owner's equity, revenue and expense. (Investopedia.com)

- **General Ledger Main Account Segment** – The segments of a general ledger account are (option 1) chart of account segment and (option2) company code segment. To keep track of financial transactions connected to a company code (CC), a general ledger is developed. The company code segment and chart of accounts segment are its two segments.(Google.com)

- **General Ledger Organization Segment** – A section (segment) of the General Ledger which includes the costs of establishing and maintaining the Firm's organization. Example: rent, utilities, travel expenses of Officers, etc.

- **General Ledger Product Segment** – In a General Ledger, a Product Segment includes the costs incurred prior to the Closing Date to bring a product to market. (CLF)

- **General Ledger Project Segment** – In a General Ledger, a Project Segment includes the costs, described in an Official Intent of the Issuer (OII), incurred prior to the Closing Date to acquire, construct, or improve land, buildings or equipment excluding current operating expenses but including costs of issuing the Reimbursement Bonds. (lawinsider.com)

- **General Ledger Sub Account Segment** – Sub accounts represent different values within a segment and along with the main account are the basic building blocks of the general ledger account. The combination of a main account and subaccounts creates a general ledger account. (Google.com)

- **Home Equity Line of Credit Agreement** – child of Loan Agreement; a contract to extend credit up to a specified amount with the borrower's home as collateral. (CLF)

- **Household** – A subtype of Customer, consisting of one or more persons occupying the same dwelling. The household is the basic unit of analysis in many social, microeconomic and government models. (Google)

- **Household Member** – An individual person who is also either a Head of Household or a member of a household/ related group living together in one dwelling. Examples include: granddaughter, Mother, Uncle, stepchild, cousin, etc. (CLF)

- **Income Statement General Ledger Main Account** - Communicates how much revenue the company generated during a period and what costs it incurred in connection with generating that revenue. The basic equation underlying the income statement, ignoring gains and losses, is Revenue minus Expenses equals Net income. (cfainstitute.org)

- **Index Fund** – A portfolio of stocks or bonds designed to mimic the composition and performance of a financial market index. (Investopedia.com)

- **Index Option** – A financial derivative that gives the holder the right, but not the obligation, to buy or sell the value of an underlying index, such as the S&P 500 index at the stated exercise price. (Google.com)

- **Individual** – A subtype of Customer, a single person doing business with a company or other legal entity of interest to the company. (CLF)

- **Individual Card** – A child of Credit Card Agreement; a credit card issued by a Bank or other Financial Institution to a single person/ individual. (CLF)

- **Individual Name** – The first, middle(s) and last legal name (appellation) of an individual, including any alternate name or nickname. (CLF)

- **Insurance Product** – A policy available for purchase through a licensed insurance agent or firm, to mitigate loss. (CLF)

- **Interest Index** - Interest that fluctuates with general market conditions. (Google.com)

- **Interest Rate** - For loans and credit cards: the proportion of a loan that is charged as interest to the borrower, typically expressed as an annual percentage of the loan outstanding. For dividends, the interest rate, expressed as a percent, is the amount paid on a stock holding on a monthly, quarterly, semi-annual or annual basis. (Investopedia.com)

- **Inventory** – A complete list of items such as property, goods in stock, or the contents of a building (Dictionary.com)

- **Investment Product** – A product purchased with the intent to grow the investment and/or receive another benefit, such as dividends or interest paid. (CLF)

- **Investment Service** - A general term used to describe a whole range of activities related to investments in financial instruments. Typically, the most common forms of investment services are the provision of investment advice and the provision of portfolio management services (collective or discretionary).(MSFA.mt)

- **ISIN Product Identifier** – An acronym for International Securities Identification Number. ISIN numbers are the unique 12-digit identification numbers recognized by the International Standards Organization (ISO) located in Geneva, Switzerland, as security identifiers for cross-border securities transactions. (Google.com)

- **Jewelry** – A subtype of Customer Asset; personal ornaments, such as necklaces, rings and bracelets,. that are typically made from or contain gems and precious metal. (Dictionary.com)

- **Journal** – A running record of all of a business's financial transactions; used to reconcile accounts and is transferred to other accounting records. (Investopedia.com)

- **Journal Entry Header** - Each journal entry contains at least one debit line item and one credit line item. In General Ledger, information that is common for each of these lines is contained in a journal entry header. The common information is entered only once for the entire transaction. (Google.com)

- **Journal Entry Line Item** - Each journal entry contains the data significant to a single business transaction, including the date, the amount to be credited and debited, a brief description of the transaction and the accounts affected. Depending on the company, it may list affected subsidiaries, tax details and other information. (Google.com)

- **Liability Account** - Used to keep track of all legally-binding debts that must be paid to someone else; a liability account records amounts owed to suppliers for goods and services that were given to you on credit. (Google.com)

- **Life Insurance** – A contract between an insurance policy holder and an insurance company, where the insurer promises to pay a sum of money in exchange for a premium, upon the death of the insured person, or after a set period of time. (Google.com)

- **Line Item** – An individual item on a Statement; an entry that appears on a separate line in a bookkeeping ledger or a fiscal budget or a purchase and sale receipt. (CLF)

- **Loan Agreement** – A child of Credit Agreement; a contract enabling the delivery of funds to the borrower, from a lender. Examples include: a loan agreement for purchase of an automobile, a loan agreement to finance the construction of a building, etc. (CLF)

- **Loan Collateral** – Real property which is promised as a guarantee that the loan will be repaid. If the loan is not repaid within the specified time frame, the property is forfeit to the lender. (CLF)

- **Location** - Comprehensive information for making contact with the legal entity; includes Physical address, telephone numbers, email address, other internet-based addresses, URLs, etc. (CLF)

- **Market Quotation** – The current price at which a stock or commodity is being traded. (lsd.law)

- **Money Market Fund** – A type of mutual fund that invests in highly liquid, near-term instruments. These instruments include cash, cash equivalent securities, and high-credit-rating, debt-based securities with a short-term maturity (such as U.S. Treasuries). (Investopedia.com)

- **Mortgage/Loan** – This entity supplies the details for either a mortgage (a loan with a house as collateral) or a loan (the borrowing of money either with or without collateral). (CLF)

- **Mortgage Loan Arrears** – When a Customer falls behind in payment on a mortgage or loan, the contract goes into "arrears" which simply means 'behind in payments.' Most firms store "arrears" as 30-day, 60-day and 90-day behind. (CLF)

- **Mortgage Loan Foreclosure** – A legal process which forces the sale of a home or other underlying asset to cover a debt. (Google)

- **Municipal Bond** - A debt security issued by states, cities, counties and other governmental entities to fund day-to-day obligations and to finance capital projects such as building schools, highways or sewer systems. (SEC.GOV)

- **Mutual Fund** - An investor's money is pooled with other investors to "mutually" buy stock, bonds and other investments. Mutual Funds usually have a particular goal and are run by professional money managers who decide which securities to buy (stocks, bonds, etc.) and when to sell them. (Google.com)

- **Option** - A financial instrument / derivative that conveys to the purchaser (the option holder) the right, but not the obligation, to buy or sell a set quantity or dollar value of a particular asset at a fixed price by a set date. (Google.com)

- **Options Contract** – An options contract gives the holder the right to buy or sell an underlying security at a preset price, known as the strike price. IGoogle.com)

- **Organization** – A subtype of Customer; a corporation, a firm, a business legally recognized by the Courts as either incorporated or LLC (Limited Liability Corporation) or DBA (Doing Business As). Basel attributes are provided for those Firms subject to Basel compliance. (CLF)

- **OTC Option** – Over the counter (OTC) options are options that are sold between private parties, usually via the broker-dealer network, rather than on exchanges. Many are smaller companies which do not meet the requirements for listing on a national exchange. (Google.com)

- **Other** – A subtype of Customer Asset; this entity is used to describe an asset which does not fall under the categories of real estate, jewelry, vehicle, inventory, equipment, vessel, animal or financial. (CLF)

- **Other Interest Rate** – An interest rate (see Rate Feature) which cannot be described as being either 'Fixed' or 'Variable;' usually constructed by a major market maker for a particular set of clients. (CLF)

- **Other Product Identifier** – A unique identifier for a financial product which is not a CUSIP or an ISIN. It may be the full name of the product, for example, 'South African Railroad Bond 2030 at 8.85%,' or another unique identifier. (CLF)

- **Other Rate Feature** – A rate structure which is neither purely fixed nor purely variable; a special, "constructed" rate feature for a financial instrument. (CLF)

- **Payment** – An amount paid by a person or company towards a debt or to settle a debt. (CLF)

- **Payment Card Product** – This entity identifies credit cards and/or banking cards used to pay bills, order products and/or access banking accounts. It is a child of Banking Product. (CLF)

- **Policy** - The resolution of the many-to-many relationship between Product and Agreement; a policy is a document detailing the terms and conditions of a contract, commonly used to describe an insurance contract/ policy. (CLF)

- **Preferred Stock** – Stock that entitles the holder to a fixed dividend, whose payment takes priority over common stock dividends. (Dictionary.com)

- **Pre-payment** – Payment of principle on a mortgage or loan before the date the payment is due. (CLF)

- **Price** – the retail cost of an item (CLF)

- **Private Equity** - Investment partnerships that buy and manage companies before selling them, (Investopedia.com)

- **Product** – An item or service offered for sale in a marketplace. Financial instruments such as savings accounts, stock, bonds, and insurance policies are examples of Products. Note that a service, such as 24x7 standby maintenance service is also a Product. (CLF)

- **Product Feature** – A resolution of the many-to-many relationship between Product and Feature, detailing which Product contains or consists of exactly which Features. (CLF)

- **Product Identification** – A unique identifier for a product; types of product identification include CUSIP, ISIN and Other. (CLF)

- **Project Task COA (Chart of Accounts)** – Information about a particular task within a General Ledger Project Segment. (CLF)

- **Property Insurance** – Provides financial reimbursement to the owner or renter of a structure and its contents in the event of damage or theft. (Investopedia.com)

- **Quantity Feature** – In a transaction, the amount being bought or sold. Examples: 100 shares of IBM, 20 government bonds, etc.(CLF)

- **Quarterly Option** – Options which are listed with expiration dates that coincide with the end of a fiscal quarter. (Google.com)

- **Rate Feature** – 1. The amount a lender charges a borrower; a percentage of the principle. 2. The percentage of return on an investment. (CLF)

- **Real Estate** – Property consisting of land and/or buildings. (Dictionary.com)

- **Real Estate Investment Trust (REIT)** – Shares in a firm that owns, manages or finances income-producing properties. (Investopedia.com)

- **Regulation** – A rule or directive made and maintained by an authority. For example: rule SEC144a (Securities and Exchange Commission) (Google)

- **Revenue Account** - Financial accounts that contain the receipts of the income or revenue that the individual or company receives through their business transactions. (Google.com)

- **Risk or Financial Risk** – the possibility or probability of losing money on an investment. (Google)

- **Role Special Instructions** - a text or list of instructions in the customer's record specifying any non-standard activity or role of the customer. For example: a note that this customer is the granddaughter of the company's founder and is entitled to a discount of 50% in the Company Store.

- **Sales Number** – A sample warehouse/ Snowflake model, designed to calculate the count of sales and a revenue amount for a particular date and time.

- **SEC Classification** - The SEC/SIC code is the Standard Industrial Classification Code which appears on the company's Edgar filings (required by the Securities and Exchange Commission) and indicates the company's type of business. Example: 6211 is the SEC/SIC code for Securities Brokers, Dealers and Flotation companies.

- o **Attribute**: SEC Classification Education Code – The 6211 code, described above, belongs in this attribute.
- **SEC144a** – Enables purchasers of securities in private placement to resell their securities to qualified institutional buyers (QIB) under certain conditions. (Investopedia.com)

- **Set of Books** - Determines the functional currency, account structure, and accounting calendar for each company or group of companies. If it is necessary to report on account balances in multiple currencies, one additional set of books for each reporting currency should be set up. (Google.com)

- **Settlement Option** – 1. In brokerage, the process for the terms of an options contract to be resolved between the relevant parties when it's exercised. 2. In Insurance, a 'settlement option' refers to the various ways in which an insurance policy's benefits can be paid out to the policy holder or to their beneficiaries. (Google.com)

- **Sinking Fund Schedule** – A sinking fund is a fund used to set aside money over time for a specific future expense A sinking fund schedule is a table that records the sinking fund contribution, the interest earned by the fund, the increase in the fund, the accumulated balance for every payment, and the current book value of the debt.. (Google.com)

- **Small Business Card** – a child of Credit Card Agreement; the type of credit card/ loan extended to a small business. Business size standards are generally based on the number of employees or the amount of annual receipts the business has. See Title 13 Part 121 of the Electronic Code of Federal Regulations(Link is external) (eCFR – U.S. Department of State).

- **Source** – The Physical starting point of a piece of financial information. Examples of sources are NYSE (The New York Stock Exchange,) the Federal Reserve Bank, Nasdaq (National Association of Securities Dealers Automated Quotations.) (CLF)

- **Statement/ Reporting** – Information to be presented to a business user in either virtual or printed form. Examples include: a Customer's monthly banking or brokerage statement, a Firm's Annual Report, an annual tax statement, etc. (CLF)

- **Status** – The standing of a person or company, usually in relation to their accounts; represented by codes, for example, 01 = Account Opened, 02 = Account in Good Standing, 03 = Account delinquent 30 days, etc. (CLF)

- **Stock** – see Common Stock

- **Stock Option** – Gives an investor the right, but not the obligation, to buy or sell a stock for a given price at an agreed upon date. (Google.com)

- **Student Card** – A child of Credit Card Agreement; a credit card issued by a Bank or Financial institution to a student of a household, who is attending High School or College. It usually has certain limits on items which can be purchased and amount spent. (CLF)

- **Swap Contract** – A swap is a derivatives contract in which one party exchanges or "swaps" the values or cash flows of one asset for another. (Investopedia.com)

- **Term Feature** – The length of time that a feature of a Financial Instrument is in effect. This entity includes several methods (attributes) for denoting the valid time period. For example, an option which has an expiration date – this is the last date a futures contract is valid. (CLF)

- **Term Life Insurance** – A life insurance product which offers financial coverage to the policyholder for a specific time period. (Google.com)

- **Time Zone** – Time zones are measured from Greenwich, U.K. and are separated by longitude lines. Each time zone has a unique name such as Eastern Standard Time (EST), Greenwich Mean Time (GMT). This information may be necessary for international transactions. (CLF)

- **Treasury Bill** – Short term debt obligations issued by the U.S. Treasury Department with a one year maturity or less. They are sold at a discount to their face value and mature at face value.

- **Treasury Note** – A marketable U.S. debt security with a fixed interest rate and a maturity of between 2 and 10 Years. (Investopedia.com)

- **Transaction** – An instance of buying or selling a product; a business deal. (Dictionary.com)

- **Universal Life Insurance** – A type of permanent life insurance that may offer adjustable premiums and an adjustable death benefit. (Allstate.com)

- **Upper Limit** – The maximum amount that a person or company is allowed to charge on their credit card or Equity Loan. (CLF)

- **U.S Treasury Bond** – Fixed rate U.S. debt securities with a maturity between 20 and 30 years. (Investopedia.com)

- **U.S. Treasury Bond Inflation Protected (TIPS)** – A type of treasury bond that is indexed to an inflationary gauge to protect investors from a decline in the purchasing power of their money. (Google.com)

- **U.S. Treasury Bond Non Inflation Protected** – A nominal bond which pays fixed interest payments based on the face value of the bond. These coupon payments do not adjust for changes in inflation. (Google.com)

- **Variable Interest Rate** – An interest rate (see Rate Feature) that can change with time, market conditions, or other event. (CLF)

- **Variable Life Insurance** - A contract between the policy holder and an insurance company. It is intended to meet certain insurance needs, investment goals, and tax planning objectives. It is a policy that pays a specified amount to the beneficiaries upon the death of the policy holder. It also has a cash value that varies according to the amount of premiums paid, the policy's fees and expenses, and the performance of a menu of investment options—typically mutual funds—offered under the policy. (Investor.gov)

- **Vehicle** – A mechanism for transporting people and/or goods, especially on land, such as a car, truck or cart. (Dictionary.com)

- **Vendor Purchase Order Line Item** – A single line of information on a purchase order to a vendor. Typically includes: a line identifier, a short description of the item being purchased, quantity, individual cost and total cost. (CLF)

- **Vessel** – a ship or large boat. (Dictionary.com)

- **Whole Life Insurance** – An insurance policy which pays a benefit on the death of the insurance and also accumulates a cash value. (Oxford Languages.com)

- **Zero Coupon Bond** – An investment in debt that does not pay interest but instead trades at a deep discount. The profit is realized at its maturity date when the bond is redeemed for its full face value. A zero coupon bond is also known as an accrual bond. (Google.com)

About the Author

Claire L. Frankel earned a Bachelor's Degree in Physics and Mathematics from the State University of New York at Albany and attended graduate school in Computer Engineering at Boston University.

She has worked as a Data Modeler, Senior Data Modeler and Executive Director of Data Modeling for 40 years at leading Banking and Wall Street financial firms. She has advised start-up companies on database technology and advised several vendors on Data Models necessary for Wall Street operations.

She is the author of white papers on SEC regulations, notably SEC 144a and b, global requirements for international firms based on the GDPR, and contributed the chapter on ANSI standards to "The Handbook for Wall Street Operations."

She lives in New York City and writes poetry for fun.

Index

www.ingramcontent.com/pod-product-compliance
Lightning Source LLC
Chambersburg PA
CBHW051759200326
41597CB00025B/4618